MORE BASKETS AND
HOW TO MAKE THEM

HANGING BASKETS

The green glass hanging vase on the left is for cut flowers. Beside it is a terra-cotta plant jar enclosed with an open weave in rattan. On the right is a brown pottery jar enclosed in heavy rings of rattan, and below it a green pottery jar for ferns has a knotted covering of bleached raffia.

More Baskets

AND

How to Make Them

By

MARY WHITE

Author of " How to Make Baskets "

*Illustrated from photographs, and drawings
by the author*

NEW YORK
DOUBLEDAY, PAGE & COMPANY
1903

To
N. de G. D.

PREFACE

THE interest in basketry which began in this country some three years ago is on the increase rather than on the wane. This may seem surprising to the uninitiated, but those who have made baskets will understand it. Basketry has proved itself. In schools and social settlements one notes the contrast between the beginners' mats and baskets, loosely woven and crude in form, and the graceful forms and solid weaving of experienced young craftsmen. A well-made basket shows more than dexterity and skill: it stands for patience and stick-to-it-iveness, and has the value of all good work. Best of all, children love the craft and would rather weave baskets or wander afield in search of natural material for weaving or dyes than do anything else you can suggest. To grown people basketry is a boon. It is unusual to find a craft so simple as to require no tools or paraphernalia, so fascinating that it never palls. Those who have tested the value and charm of basketry, the many friends who have learned with me how to make baskets, will, I trust, be as glad to receive as I am to send them a few more baskets.

CONTENTS

LIST OF ILLUSTRATIONS
(Half-tones)

LIST OF FIGURES

LIST OF FIGURES (*Continued*)

Centres and Weaves

MORE BASKETS AND HOW TO MAKE THEM

CHAPTER I

CENTRES AND WEAVES

TO begin with the centre seems natural, since it is the starting point of all round baskets.

The centres and weaves in this chapter are intended especially for rattan basketry; others for raffia baskets will be found in Chapter VIII. We shall use the simple centre described in "How to Make Baskets" so seldom that it seems hardly necessary to repeat the directions for it. The sixteen-spoke centre, however, is so generally used in beginning the baskets in this book that it will be wise, perhaps, to review it.

Sixteen spokes are cut from rattan of the size required, No. 2 for small baskets, No. 3 for medium sizes, and No. 4 or No. 5 for scrap-baskets, large trays, etc.

The weaver used is of the same size as the spokes. The spokes having been wet until pliable, are separated into fours, and the approximate centre found by bending each group so that the ends touch. The first four is laid on a table, or other flat surface, in a vertical position. Across this group, at the centre, four horizontal spokes are laid, then a diagonal four, from the right of the upper vertical spokes to the left of the lower ones. The remaining four spokes are laid across the centre diagonally, in the opposite direction, completing the star shape (see Fig. 1). A weaver is started under the horizontal spokes on the left and brought over the next group, under the next, and so on. In the second row the weaver is brought under and over the same groups as in the first. The third and fourth rows also follow, making a band of four rows which corresponds with the

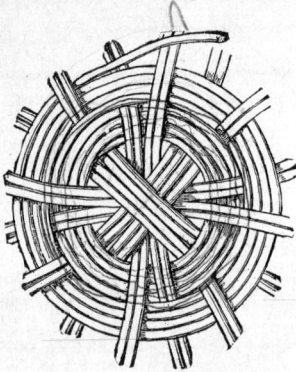

Fig. 1

groups of four spokes. At the end of the fourth row the groups are separated into twos, bringing the weaver under the first two of the horizontal spokes on the left, over the next, and so on, making a fifth row. If a small centre is desired, the weaver passes under two groups of spokes at the beginning of the sixth row. In making a large centre the sixth row of weaving follows the fifth row, as does the seventh and eighth. At the beginning of the ninth row the weaver passes under two groups of spokes. This process, which was alluded to in "How to Make Baskets," is one the Indians follow in using under-and-over weaving on an even number of spokes. At the beginning of each new row the weaver passes under

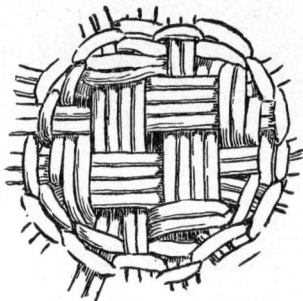

Fig. 2

two spokes, or groups of spokes, as the case may be; always under the last of the two spokes it went under in the previous row and the one to the right of it.

Another sixteen-spoke centre is made by crossing the four groups of spokes, which should be perfectly pliable, as in Fig. 2. The first group is laid on a table vertically, the second crosses it horizontally. The third group is laid across the second vertically, and the fourth crosses the third horizontally and slips under the lower end of the first group. The end of a pliable weaver is laid under the left end of the fourth group, with its tip turning down, and is woven over the next group, under the next, and so on. It is brought around a second time, following the first row, to bind the spokes. A third row of weaving then separates the spokes into groups of two and the weaving continues, following the Indian process for an even number of spokes.

An openwork centre is sometimes desirable. The Indians make one that is absolutely simple (see Fig. 3). The original was made with willow twigs, and we can copy it in the same material or in No. 4 rattan bound with pairing in No. 2. Four vertical spokes are laid across four horizontal ones which are placed an eighth of an inch apart. A row of pairing started at the upper left hand corner of the centre and carried around it holds the

spokes firmly in place. At each of the four
corners an additional spoke is inserted, and the
rest of the basket is woven in rows of pairing
about a quarter of an
inch apart.

Moki Centre.—The
plaques or trays made
by the Moki Indians
are woven in under-and-
over weaving, and their
centres will often sug-
gest ways of starting
rattan baskets. One

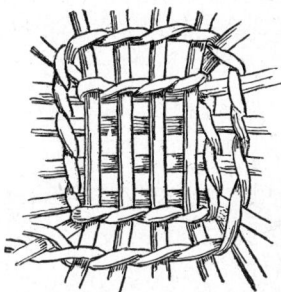

FIG. 3

such centre is made as follows: Twelve spokes
of No. 4 rattan are to be bound together
with No. 2 split rattan. One spoke is held
in the hand and an end of the split rattan
is wound around it. Another spoke is then
bound beside it, the weaver passing around
the two spokes. Then another, the weaver passing
around three, and so on. When the weaver has
passed around all six spokes it is brought once
around the sixth spoke, above the last binding
(see Fig. 4), then around two, and so on, filling up
the other half of the square. When this is done

the other six spokes are bound in the same way (back of the first six and crossing them at right angles) with the same weaver, which may afterward be used to separate the spokes enough to allow for weaving with round rattan.

Another Moki centre is as attractive as it is simple. Some pliable material, preferably fine rush, may be used for the weaver on spokes of No. 2 rattan. There are eighteen spokes in the centre, nine in each group. These groups are subdivided into threes. A pliable weaver of the rush is started around one of the groups of three, woven under the next group and around the third. In returning, it is brought over the middle group and around the group where it started. Thus it goes on; under-and-over weaving binds the spokes together for six rows, or twelve times back and forth. The other set of spokes is bound in the

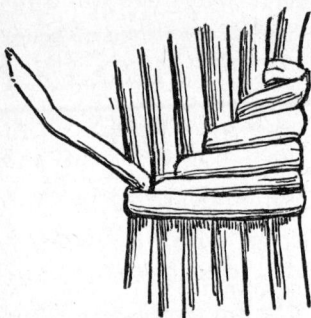

Fig. 4

same way and laid horizontally back of the first set, which is held in a vertical position, and the two are bound together as the weaving proceeds (see Fig. 5).

Italian Centre.—An elaborate and effective centre is copied from an Italian basket. The original was made with a material like broom-straw, but it may be copied in No. 2 rattan or even No. 1. Sixty spokes of the required length are cut, and these are separated into four groups of fifteen each. The first arrangement is not unlike the sixteen-spoke centre shown in Fig. 2, except that the first group laid on the table or other flat surface is in a horizontal position. The next group crosses the first vertically, at the left of the exact centre. The third is laid across the second horizontally, and the

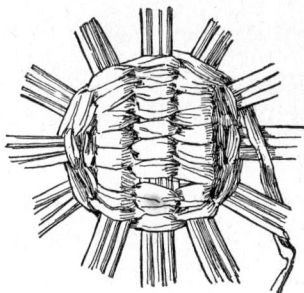

FIG. 5

fourth crosses the third vertically and slips under the right end of the first group. Back of the first three spokes in the upper end of the second group the first three in the upper end of the fourth group are brought, and a weaver of the same size as the spokes is doubled around them and woven in pairing each time, enclosing six spokes, three from

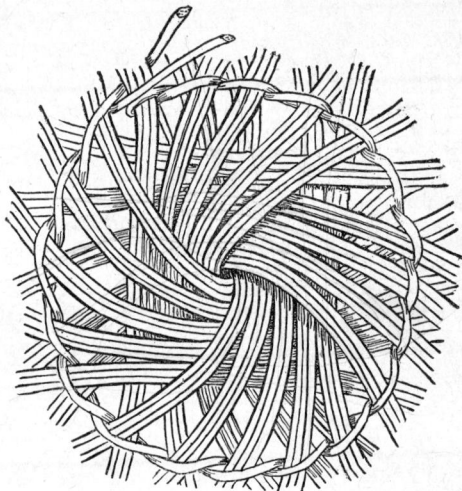

FIG. 6

each of these groups (see Fig. 6).   It next encloses three spokes at a time from the right end of the first group, with three from the right end of the third group.   Then groups of three from the lower end of the fourth group are enclosed with threes from the lower end of the second.   Last the groups of three in the left end of the third group are enclosed with threes from the left end of the first group, completing the circuit. The bottom of the original basket was woven with groups of two weavers in pairing, and the sides

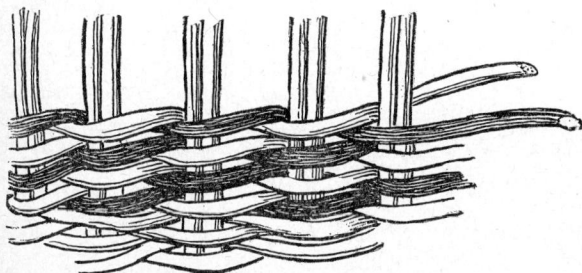

Fig. 7

were made with groups of three weavers, nine in all, in triple twist, each group passing over three groups of spokes and under two.

Effective bands and designs in colour may be made on rattan baskets with the simple weaves described in "How to Make Baskets." Rows of pairing on an uneven number of spokes with weavers of different colours on a basket of the natural colour form bands. If one weaver is of the natural colour and one of an effective contrasting colour (either a bright or a deep shade), diagonal lines on a background of the natural colour will result (see Fig. 7). Two weavers of different colours woven in pairing on an even number of spokes make coloured lines down the basket, like vertical stripes. If a checker effect is desired, after weaving four or five rows of pairing with weavers of different colours, in beginning a new row each weaver is brought behind two spokes. This makes each colour come above the contrasting one. Four rows are woven in this way, and then at the beginning of the next row each weaver is brought back of two spokes, which again changes the weave (see Fig. 8).

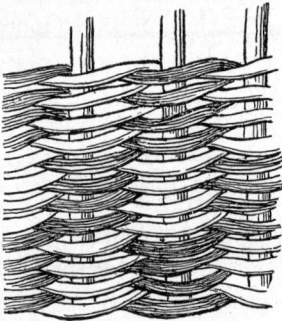

Fig. 8

A great variety of effects may be obtained by using the triple twist in different combinations of colour. Diagonal lines longer and more slanting than those made with pairing are woven with triple twist on baskets of the natural colour by taking one weaver of a dark or bright colour and two of the natural colour (see Fig. 9). To accomplish this on an uneven number of spokes each weaver is brought behind two spokes at the beginning of every new row. In order to make diagonal lines on an even number no change is necessary. Two weavers of the darker colour with one of the natural makes an effective band if four or more rows are woven. An arrowhead design is made by

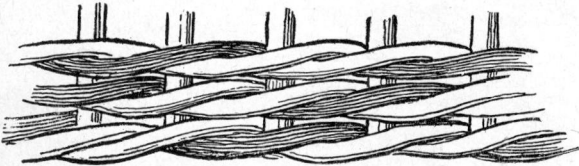

FIG. 9

weaving three or four rows in this way and then, at the beginning of a row, a weaver of the natural colour is started back of the spoke behind which the first weaver of the natural colour ended, with its tip toward the right. A weaver of the contrasting colour is started behind the next spoke to the left and another behind the spoke following it, and the triple twist is woven to the left for the same number of rows as it was woven to the right, reversing the design (see Fig. 10.)

Triple Braid.—A charming weave that is found on Japanese baskets is not as difficult as it looks. It is most successfully done with flat material—

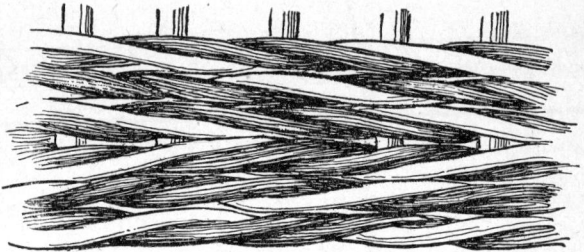

FIG. 10

split rattan, cane or silver top (see Chapter X.). As in triple twist, three weavers start behind three successive spokes and are brought in turn, begin-

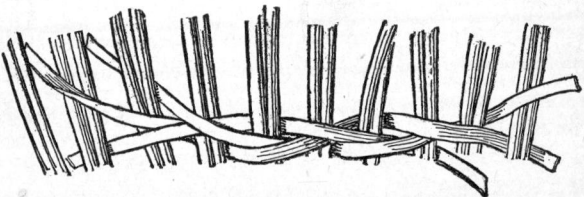

FIG. 11

ning with the back one, over two and under one spoke, but there the similarity ends. Instead of twisting, the weavers form a braid. The first weaver is made to slant downward as it passes over two spokes and back of one, but instead of passing over the other two weavers, as in triple twist, it should come out between them. The next weaver is brought upward over two and back of one spoke, and that also ends between the other two weavers. The third weaver is brought downward, over two and back of one spoke, ending between the other weavers. Thus it goes on; if one weaver is brought upward the following one comes down, and each ends between the other two (see Fig. 11).

Flower Baskets

CHAPTER II

FLOWER BASKETS.

THE high-handled flower basket of our grandmother's time is seldom seen nowadays except in pictures. It has gone the way of the old-fashioned bouquet with short-stemmed flowers tightly bound together. In gathering masses of long-stemmed roses from our gardens we shall find a tray-shaped basket more convenient.

Rose Tray of Green Rattan

Materials: 16 34-inch pieces of No. 4 green rattan,
32 16-inch pieces of No. 4 green rattan,
About 16 weavers of No. 4 green rattan,
An awl.

One of the recipes for green dye given in Chapter X. may be used to colour the weavers and spokes before this basket is made, or it may be stained after it is finished with green wood stain, according to the directions in Chapter XII. of "How to Make Baskets." The large sixteen-spoke centre is made (see Fig. 1) and then the weaving is continued, keeping the bottom perfectly flat, for seven and

19

three-quarters inches.   Additional spokes are here inserted, two between each pair of spokes, using an awl to separate them.   When three rows more have been woven the sides are turned upward with a very gradual flare for three and a half inches. The tray shape should be kept in mind always. The basket will then be fifteen and a half inches across, measuring on the outside.   Here the spokes are wet and turned sharply in and an inch and three-quarters of weaving with a tightly drawn weaver is made.   The edge is then bound off and the following border completes the tray.   In the first row each group of spokes is brought back of the next group on the right and out.   In the second row each group of ends is brought over the next group of spokes (above the next group of ends) and in.   The third row is made by bringing each group of ends back of the next group of spokes and outside, below the border, where they are cut just long enough to allow each to lie against the next group of spokes.

Basket Fern Dish

Materials: 16 46-inch spokes of No. 4 green rattan,
8 weavers of No. 4 natural-coloured rattan,
1 weaver of No. 4 green rattan,
An awl.

FLOWER BASKETS

The rose-tray on the left and above the others is woven in green and the natural colour; under it is a larger basket tray with outside spokes of a deeper shade of green. The basket fern-dish beside it is of green and the natural colour; while the tray behind it and the openwork basket for violets on the right are of green rattan.

An attractive centrepiece for ferns is woven of rattan in green combined with the natural colour. The green rattan may be dyed or stained, but the shade should be deep enough to contrast with the natural colour of rattan. The spokes, which are of No. 4 green rattan forty-six inches long, are arranged in the usual sixteen-spoke centre, and the weaver, after four rows have been woven, following under and over the same spokes as the first row, is brought under the first pair of horizontal spokes on the left, over the next pair, and so on, separating the groups of four into twos. At the beginning of the sixth row the weaver passes under two pairs of spokes, and the rest of the basket is woven according to the Indian method for an even number of spokes, described in Chapter I. When the bottom is seven inches in diameter the sides are turned up, with a very gradual flare, for two inches and a half. The spokes are then wet and rounded in toward the centre by bending them over the finger. One inch more is woven, drawing the spokes in closer. The basket is then bound off at the top and the following border woven: Each group of spokes is brought over the next two groups on the right,

under the next group and outside.   The basket is
then turned upside down, and with the help of an
awl each group of ends is brought through a row
of weaving about three and a half inches from the
centre just in front of the next spoke to the last
one it went under.   Two rows of weaving with a
weaver of No. 4 green rattan are made, to separate
the ends of the spokes and form the beginning of a
base, which is completed by bringing each pair of
ends over the next pair on the right and inside
of the base, where they are cut short.   **A** white
enameled baking-dish may be bought to fit this
basket, and ferns planted in it.   It makes a charming fern basket, and a practical one, for water will
not injure any part of it.

Green Openwork Basket for Violets

Materials: 24 30-inch pieces of No. 2 rattan,
2 weavers of No. 2 rattan,
An iridescent glass bowl.

Nothing could be more harmonious than the cool
green of this open-meshed basket enclosing an
iridescent glass bowl filled with violets. The
basket is dainty, yet very simply made. The
arrangement of spokes in the usual sixteen-spoke
centre is followed, except that there are six spokes

in each of the four groups, instead of four, and the weaver follows three times around these groups before they are separated into threes. Ten rows of under-and-over weaving, according to the Indian method, for an even number of spokes, make a slightly rounded bottom. The edge is bound off, and each group of spokes having been wet until pliable, is brought under the next group on the right, over the next, under the next, over the next, under the next and outside. The mat-shaped basket is then moulded up between the hands into a bowl shape, like the openwork candy basket in "How to Make Baskets." The spokes are drawn in or out and the top pressed closely in until it fits the glass bowl. This process will take time and patience, for the edge of the basket should be even and on a line with the edge of the bowl. When this is accomplished the basket is turned upside down and a pliable weaver doubled around one of the groups of ends is woven in pairing for two rows to form part of a base. This should be done carefully so as not to draw the ends too close together and make the finishing of the base difficult. Each group of ends is then brought over the next two groups, on the left and inside the base, which completes it. In order to get the silvery green colour for this basket, it is not soaked in the alum mordant before dyeing (see Chapter X.), but simply wet in clear water. The directions for green dye with indigo and bark extract may be used, but before dyeing it the colour should be tried on bits of rattan.

Rose Tray in Green and Natural Colour

Materials: 16 40-inch spokes of No. 4 green rattan,
32 16-inch spokes of No. 4 green rattan,
About 6 weavers of No. 4 natural-coloured rattan,
10 or 12 weavers of No. 4 green rattan,
An awl.

Sixteen spokes of green rattan are arranged in the centre, shown in Figure 1, which is made with the four-row beginning. An inch and a quarter is woven in green, and then a weaver of the natural colour follows for four rows, under and over the same spokes, to make an ornamental band. Six rows of green are woven, changing the weave with each row in the usual way. At this point, when the bottom is seven and a quarter inches in diameter, the extra spokes are inserted, two between each pair. They are separated into twos and the weaving continues for seven rows in under-and-over weaving. Two weavers of green rattan and one of the natural colour are woven in four rows of triple twist; the spokes are then wet until pliable and turned upward in a gradual flare. Four rows of under-and-over weaving in green are made. Just here it may be said that in turning up baskets of this kind—tray-shaped and having the decoration on the bottom—the usual rule of turning the spokes away from the worker (so that the side toward one is the outside of the basket) need not be adhered to. The basket may be turned over, the last weaver cut back of a spoke and a new one started going from left to right, as one holds what was the inside of the basket toward one. This brings all the joinings and the rope-like ridge (formed by skipping back of two spokes at the beginning of each row) on the outside of the bottom of the basket, and on the inside of the sides. To return to the basket tray we are weaving: Seven rows more of green rattan are woven, still flaring the sides. Then four rows of the natural colour under and over the same spokes, to form a band, two rows of green, and the spokes are wet and turned sharply in. A weaver of the natural colour is

started and the weave is changed in every other
row so that the effect is like double weaving.   Ten
rows are woven in this way, drawing the spokes in
more and more.   The edge is finished with this
border: Each pair of spokes is brought over
the next pair, under the next, over the next, under
the next, over the next and inside the basket,
where they are cut.

Large Basket Tray for Fruit or Flowers

Materials: 16 56-inch spokes of No. 5 green rattan,
   32 25-inch spokes of No. 5 green rattan,
   18 or 20 weavers of No. 5 rattan in the
      natural colour,
   An awl.

Another tray-shaped basket is appropriate for
gathering flowers, or it may be used on a piazza
to hold fruit.   Against the soft green of its border
masses of nasturtiums or clusters of grapes would
be most effective.   It is strong and capacious and
admirably adapted for use in a country house.
The spokes are dyed with the recipe for dark
bluish-green in Chapter X.   Sixteen spokes
are started, as in Figure 1, and the four-row
beginning is made with a weaver of the
natural colour.   When the bottom is seven

and a half inches in diameter the extra spokes are inserted, two between each pair. These are again separated into twos, and when the bottom is twelve inches in diameter the spokes are turned up and flared outward for three and a quarter inches. They are then wet until pliable and bent in toward the centre by rounding them over the finger. A tightly drawn weaver brings the spokes closer together with each row until an inch and a half has been woven, when the edge is bound off and the following border made: Each pair of spokes is brought over the next two pairs, under the next and outside. The basket is then turned upside down and each pair of ends is brought through a row of weaving about six inches from the centre and in front of the next pair of spokes to the pair it went behind. Two rows of under-and-over weaving in No. 5 green rattan form the beginning of a base, and each pair of ends is brought over the next pair and inside of the base, completing the basket.

Baskets for Practical Use

CHAPTER III

"WHAT is it for?" is asked so often that one realizes utility is the first requisite of a basket. Strong and well-made and adapted to its place in the household it must be, and it should be beautiful and harmonious as well.

String Basket of Orange and Black Rattan

Materials : 16 24-inch pieces of No. 2 orange rattan,
9 or 10 weavers of No. 2 orange rattan,
3 weavers of No. 2 black rattan.

Sixteen twenty-four-inch pieces of No. 2 orange rattan are arranged in the centre, shown in Figure 1. The four-row beginning is woven, and when the centre is four inches in diameter the sides are rounded up, flaring them outward decidedly for an inch and three-quarters. An inch more is woven, drawing the spokes in gradually more and more and the spokes are bent in toward the centre. Two weavers of black rattan and one of the orange are then woven in four rows of triple twist, drawing them tightly.   The ends of these weavers are cut about half an inch beyond the point on the circumference of the basket where the triple twist was started, and after wetting them until pliable each is run down between the weaving beside a spoke. The border is made as follows: In the first row each pair of spokes is brought over the next two pairs, under the next pair and outside.   The ends are drawn tightly, making the border open.   In the second row each pair of ends is brought over the next pair of spokes and inside, where they are cut so as to allow each to lie against the pair of spokes in front.

Duster Case

Materials: 6 36-inch pieces of No. 2 rattan,
2 or 3 weavers of No. oo rattan,
6 large dark-blue beads,
6 large iridescent beads,
A Japanese duster with silk top.

A Japanese duster with bamboo handle and top of soft silk cut in narrow strips is most decorative.   It is of practical value, too, in keeping polished mahogany furniture free from dust. This quiver-shaped basket makes an appropriate case for it.   Six spokes of No. 2 rattan thirty-six inches long are crossed in the centre and bound twice with a weaver of No. oo before the under-

and-over weaving (in the Indian method for an even number of spokes, see Chapter I.) is begun. A centre one inch in diameter is woven and then the spokes are wet and turned up with straight sides for two inches and a quarter. A dark-blue bead is slipped on to every other spoke, and the weaver having been pushed up through one of these beads, the end of another weaver is run down beside the next spoke on the right and two rows of pairing are woven. The spokes are then brought straight up without weaving for two inches and a half. Here a weaver doubled around a spoke is woven in two rows of pairing. Again the spokes are brought up straight without weaving for four and three-quarters inches, when a piece of weaver is doubled around a spoke and one row of pairing is woven. On every other spoke an iridescent bead is threaded and the weavers are brought up through two successive beads to be woven in two more rows of pairing. Again the spokes are brought up without weaving for an inch and seven-eighths, when seven-eighths of an inch of pairing is woven and the following border made: In the first row each spoke is brought back of the spoke on the right and outside. In the second row each end is brought around back of the next

spoke and outside, down by the weaving. As it
is brought through in this way it lies close to
another end, which it
should precede, so
that the next end to
take will always be
the back one of the
pair thus formed. A
ring to hang it by
is made by passing a
piece of No. oo rattan,
about eighteen inches
long, back of two
spokes between the last two rows of weaving and
tying it into a ring (see Fig. 12). The ends are
twisted in and out around the foundation ring
twice, making three circuits, which complete it.

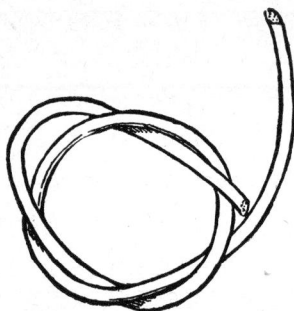

FIG. 12

Work-Basket with Checker Design in Olive-Green and Yellow

Materials: 16 30-inch pieces of No. 2 rattan,
32 14-inch pieces of No. 2 rattan,
8 weavers of No. 2 rattan,
4 or 5 weavers of No. 2 olive-green rattan,
3 weavers of No. 2 yellow rattan,
An awl.

Sixteen spokes of No. 2 rattan are separated into
four groups of four each and arranged in the centre,
shown in Figure 2. After they are bound, seven
rows of under-and-over weaving are made, using the
Indian method for an even number of spokes. A
band of four rows without changing the weave is
followed by nine rows of under-and-over weaving,
changing the weave as usual at the beginning of
each row.

Here the extra spokes are inserted, two
between each pair of spokes, and six rows more
are woven.

A band of checker design is now started
with a weaver of olive-green and one of
yellow. Two rows of pairing are made. At the
beginning of the third row each weaver passes
behind two pairs of spokes and the pairing continues for four rows. At the beginning of the
seventh row each weaver is brought back of two
pairs of spokes, and two more rows are made. The
under-and-over weaving in the natural colour is
now resumed, and the spokes are wet and turned
up, flaring outward.

As in the basket tray described in Chapter
II., the spokes may be turned up toward the

person weaving, so that the side toward one becomes the inside (instead of the outside) of the basket. If this is to be done, the weaver is cut back of a pair of spokes at the beginning of the eighth row from the coloured band. Anotl er weaver is started with its long end to the right and its tip back of a pair of spokes and the weaving proceeds, the sides still flaring decidedly, for an inch. Here the spokes are wet and bent in toward the centre. A weaver of green and one of yellow, quite tightly drawn, are woven in pairing for two rows. At the beginning of the third row each weaver passes back of two pairs of spokes and three rows of pairing follow. At the beginning of the sixth row each weaver passes back of two pairs of spokes, and two more rows of pairing complete the band. Five rows of under-and-over weaving in the natural colour draw the spokes closer. A band of three rows in olive-green, without changing the weave, is followed by two rows of under-and-over weaving in the natural colour. The edge is bound off and finished with this border: Each pair of spokes is brought under the next two pairs, over the next pair, under the next, over the next and inside of the basket.

Hairpin Basket in Two Shades of Green

Materials: 16 16-inch pieces of No. 2 olive-green rattan,
4 or 5 weavers of No. 2 pale-green rattan.

A basket to hold hairpins on the dressing-table
will be found useful.

A weaver of pale-green rattan is started, on a
sixteen-spoke centre of olive-green spokes, in the
four-row beginning and woven into a bottom
four inches in diameter. The spokes are then
wet and turned up with a decided flare and three-
quarters of an inch of weaving is made. After
turning the spokes in by rounding them over the
finger, two rows of weaving draw them in gradually
more and more. Four rows are woven without
changing the weave, making an ornamental band.
Three rows more of the under-and-over weaving
are followed by four rows without changing the
weave. Five rows of under-and-over weaving
draw the spokes in closer. The edge is then
bound off and the following border completes it:
After the spokes are wet until pliable each group is
brought under the first group on the right, over the
next and inside the basket, where each is cut just
long enough to allow it to rest on the spoke ahead.

Indian Shaped Scrap Basket

Materials: 8 42-inch spokes of No. 5 rattan,
     1 22-inch spoke of No. 5 rattan,
     16 18-inch spokes of No. 5 rattan,
     About 40 weavers of No. 4 rattan,
     About 3 weavers of No. 4 black rattan,
     About 4 weavers of No. 4 Indian red rattan,
     An awl.

Four of the eight long spokes are slit in the centre for about an inch. Through these slits the other four long spokes and the one twenty-two-inch spoke are run. A weaver of No. 4 rattan is started back of the slit spokes, with its tip toward the right. It is brought around in front of those spokes, down back of the four on the right, and over the lower end of the slit spokes. It is then brought up diagonally back of the centre to the right of the upper end of the slit spokes, over the spokes on the right, up diagonally back of the centre to the left of the upper end of the slit spokes. Then down in front of the spokes on the left, back of the lower end of the slit spokes, where it passes out and around the first spoke in the group and the weaving begins. A flat bottom seven and a quarter inches in diameter is woven, and then, with the aid of an awl, the extra spokes are inserted, one on the

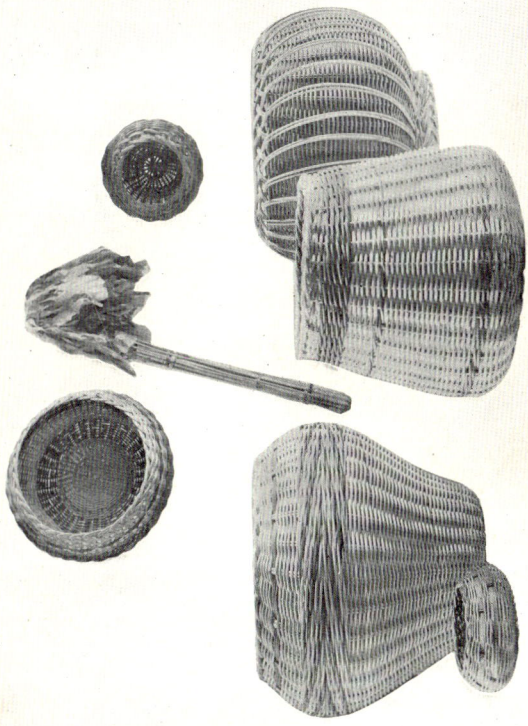

BASKETS FOR PRACTICAL USE

Beside the work-basket, with checker design, is a duster case with bead decoration. On the right is a string basket in orange and black. The green scrap-basket below, with spokes of the natural colour has beside it one with a band in Indian red and black. The vase-shaped scrap-basket has a design in black. The small hairpin basket is of pale-green rattan.

right of each of the original spokes except one
(to keep the uneven number), where the spokes are
close together. The spokes are then separated
and when the bottom is eight inches in diameter
they are wet and turned upward with a flare for
two inches. Next the spokes are rounded inward
and drawn together slightly, while three-quarters
of an inch is woven. A weaver of Indian red
rattan and one of black make two rows of pairing.
Four inches of under-and-over weaving in the
natural colour draw the sides of the basket in
gradually. One row of pairing follows in black
and Indian red. An inch and a quarter of under-
and-over weaving in the natural colour is followed
by a band made of five rows of triple twist, with
two weavers of No. 4 Indian red rattan and one
of black. At the beginning of the second and
every succeeding row each weaver passes behind
two spokes, which changes the weave so that
diagonal lines of black show on a background of
Indian red, making an effective decoration. Four
rows of under-and-over weaving in the natural
colour are followed by the binding and this border:
A small piece is cut from the right side of each
spoke close to the weaving. The spokes are wet

until pliable, when each is brought back of the next two spokes on the right and outside. In the second row each end is brought over the next two spokes on the right, above the ends, and pushed inside the basket, where it is cut long enough to allow it to rest on the spoke ahead.

Scrap Basket of Rattan in Green and the Natural Colour

> **Materials :** 16 70-inch pieces of No. 4 rattan,
> 32 32-inch pieces of No. 4 rattan,
> About 45 weavers of No. 4 rattan,
> An awl.

An effective scrap basket is made on the same principle as the knitting basket in "How to Make Baskets."

Sixteen spokes are arranged as in Figure 1. The eight-row beginning is made and a centre eight inches in diameter is woven. Here the extra spokes are inserted, two between each group. The groups are separated into twos and the basket shaped as nearly round as possible. At the widest point the circumference should be thirty-eight inches; from there it is gradually drawn in until the diameter of the top is about ten and a half inches. At this point the basket is bound off and stained green with wood-stain, just to the edge of the weaving, leaving the long spokes in the natural colour. A weaver is also stained. When the stain is dry the spokes are wet until pliable. Each group of spokes is brought over the next two groups on the right, under the third group and outside. The basket is then turned upside down and each group of spokes is brought to the bottom of the basket, about where the extra spokes were inserted and in front of the next spoke to the one it last went behind. Here it is drawn through a row of weaving to hold it in place. These outside groups should be left quite loose. Two rows of under-and-over weaving in green rattan make part of a base; the end of each group is then brought under the next two groups on the right, over the next two and pressed down inside, completing the base.

Large Scrap Basket with Arrowhead Design
in Black

Materials: 16 50-inch spokes of No. 5 rattan,
32 23-inch spokes of No. 5 rattan,
About 45 weavers of No. 4 rattan,
About 8 weavers of No. 4 black rattan,
An awl.

A vase-shaped scrap basket is woven of rattan in the natural colour, with an arrowhead design in black. The spokes are of No. 5 rattan and the weavers of No. 4. The eight-row beginning is made on the usual sixteen-spoke centre. When the centre is six and a half inches in diameter, the extra spokes are inserted, two between each pair of the original spokes. When the bottom measures seven and a quarter inches in diameter the spokes are wet until pliable and turned up almost at right angles with it. The sides are woven for two inches, keeping the spokes nearly straight, then they are flared very slightly, while two inches more are woven. Four inches are made, flaring the sides still more. The spokes are now wet and bent in gradually. Two weavers of the natural colour and one of black rattan are started in triple twist, and five rows are woven, drawing the spokes in slightly. At the end of the fifth row the basket should measure forty-six and a half inches in circumference—the widest point. Each weaver is now cut back of a spoke and started again behind the same spoke with its long end toward the left. Five more rows are woven from right to left, reversing the design and drawing the spokes in still more. An inch and three-eighths of under-and-over weaving, drawn closely, is followed by three rows of black without changing the weave. One inch of under-and-over weaving draws the spokes in still more, then the edge is bound off and the following border made: After the spokes have been wet until pliable a small piece is cut from the right side of each, close to the weaving. In the first row each pair of spokes is brought back of the next two pairs on the right and outside. In the second row each pair of ends is brought over the next pair of spokes, above the next pair of ends, and pushed inside, where they are cut just long enough to rest on the pair ahead.

Hanging Baskets

CHAPTER IV

HANGING BASKETS

CHARMING effects may be obtained by incasing pottery and glass jars for plants and flowers with knotted raffia or open-meshed weaves in rattan. Here is a wide field for the original craftsman. A few of the possibilities are suggested in the following pages. Some hanging baskets of rattan are also described.

Hanging Jar for Ferns

Materials: A green pottery jar 9 inches in circumference at the top, 14 inches at the widest part, 10⅞ inches in circumference at the bottom and 3½ inches high,
A bunch of bleached raffia.

The bleached raffia sold by dealers in florists' supplies looks most attractive over the dull-green of this pottery jar. Three strands of raffia are braided for nine and a half inches in the middle of the strands. The six ends are brought together, one is cut short and the other five are

braided in a flat plait for an inch and a half. Five
and a half inches are left loose and then four and
a half inches are braided in a flat plait, joining
new strands as they are needed according to
directions in Chapter VII. Another five and a
half inches are left loose and an inch and a half is
braided in a flat plait. The end is then attached
to the narrow braid exactly opposite the point
where the broad plait began. This makes a ring
of narrow braiding to slip over the top of the jar
and a broad plait for the flexible handle. Sixteen
strands are knotted on the narrow ring (see directions for knotting in "How to Make Baskets").
At about half an inch from the top the first row
of knots is made. Another row of knotting at
half an inch from the first row, separating the
strands, makes half of a diamond-shaped mesh.
In the third row the strands are brought down
together and knotted at two inches from the
previous row. Here they are separated again
and two rows of knotting in the diamond-shaped
mesh are made half an inch apart. The bottom-
less bag thus formed is wet, slipped over the top
of the jar and fitted close to it. A double strand
of raffia is run through the last row of diamond-

shaped meshes and tied securely. This should come under the jar at about an inch from the edge. The ends of the strands are cut close to the last row of knots, completing the covering.

Brown Pottery Jar Incased in Rattan Rings

Materials: A brown pottery jar 2 inches in diameter at the top, 3⅛ inches high and 3⅛ inches in diameter at the bottom,
4 weavers of No. 4 rattan,
A bunch of raffia,
A tapestry needle No. 19.

The Chinese sometimes suspend ginger jars in a quaint casing formed by five rings of rattan. It is simply made as follows: Five pieces of No. 4 rattan about forty-four inches long are tied into rings (see Fig. 12) three inches in diameter, making three circuits on each ring, counting the foundation ring as one circuit. Four of these rings make the sides and the fifth forms the bottom. Each one of the four rings is bound to the next one with three-quarters of an inch of raffia in buttonhole stitch, the four forming a hollow square. A fifth ring is bound at the bottom to each of the others with three-quarters of an inch of raffia in button-hole stitch. The jar is then slipped into this

open case and a handle is made as follows: Half
a length of No. 4 rattan is tied through two of the
rings above a joining to form a small ring. The
ends are brought through this ring and up, making
a half circuit with each. They are now twisted
together for fourteen inches to the point diagonally
opposite where the other two rings are joined. Here
they are tied back of the joining, and on the imper-
fect ring thus formed one of the ends is twisted in
and out until it has made the circuit and returned
to the other end back of the joining, where both
are cut just long enough to lie against a coil of the
ring.

Green Glass Hanging Vase

Materials: A dark-green hyacinth glass,
2 weavers of No. 2 rattan,
2 weavers of No. 2 black rattan,
A bunch of copper-red raffia,
A tapestry needle No. 19.

Rings of rattan in the natural colour and black
suspend this vase. It is a dark-green hyacinth
glass, such as may be obtained at any large seed
store. The binding of copper-red raffia is just
what is needed to complete a colour scheme which
suggests Austrian glass. White flowers—carna-
tions, chrysanthemums or roses—look well in it.

Two rings of black rattan are made, one large enough to slip down to about half an inch from the bottom of the vase, the other to three inches from the bottom. This second ring must be made on the vase, as the flaring top will not allow so small a ring to slip over it. For method of making these rings see Figure 12. They are twisted in and out twice around the foundation ring, making three circuits. Other rings two and a quarter inches in diameter, inside measurement, are made of the natural-coloured rattan with two circuits. These are bound, between the black ones and to each other (securing the ends by making the binding come over them), around the vase with copper-red raffia, in buttonhole stitch, for five-eighths of an inch at each binding. A simple way is to bind the four together in a hollow square which will slip over the top of the vase, and may then be bound to the upper and lower black rings. Another ring of black, made with three circuits, is tied around the neck of the vase and its ends made into a ring an inch and a quarter in diameter inside measurement, which stands out from the vase and acts as a loop to hang it by. This ring is made with two circuits.

Pottery Jar with Rattan Covering

Materials: A pottery jar 18½ inches in circumference at
the top, 5¾ inches high and 3¼ inches in
circumference at the base,
8 26-inch spokes of No. 4 rattan,
1 14-inch spoke of No. 4 rattan,
4 weavers of No. 2 rattan,
1 weaver of No. 2 black rattan,
3 pieces of No. 4 rattan 46 inches long,
A piece of wire,
A pair of pliers,
2 or 3 strands of raffia.

The simple centre shown in Figure 10 of "How
to Make Baskets" is used in starting the four-inch
bottom of the basket covering with which this
plant jar is enclosed. The sides, very slightly
flared, are woven for five-eighths of an inch in
under-and-over weaving.   A weaver of No. 2
black rattan is then cut into three pieces and
woven in one row of triple twist. One row of
pairing in the natural colour follows. The spokes
are wet thoroughly, and the pottery jar, having
been set into the shallow basket already woven,
openwork sides are made as follows: Every other
spoke is brought to the right and the alternate
ones to the left (on the principle of the Indian stitch
shown in Figure 42 of "How to Make Baskets"),
to a distance of three and three-quarters inches

from the last row of weaving, where (each having diagonally crossed two of the alternate spokes) they are held by two rows of pairing in No. 2 rattan of the natural colour. To finish the edge the end of each spoke which was brought to the right is pushed down through the two stitches of pairing to the right of it and up through the next two, where it is cut short. The end of each spoke which was brought to the left is pushed down through the two stitches of pairing to the left of it, up through the next two, and is there cut short. Three pieces of No. 4 rattan forty-six inches long form the handle. Back of the crossing of two of the diagonal spokes, just below the last two rows of pairing, one of these forty-six-inch pieces of rattan is brought. The ends are twisted together for nine and three-quarters inches, where they are tied, temporarily, with a piece of raffia. Another piece of rattan is brought back of the third crossing of spokes from the one back of which the first piece was brought.

The ends of this piece are also twisted together and tied in with the ends of the first piece. The third piece is brought back of the third crossing of spokes to the right of the one where the second was brought through, and the ends of this piece are twisted for nine and three-quarters inches.   Here all the ends are bound securely with wire and, after wetting them until they are pliable, all six ends are twisted together for nine inches and bent into a loop, which is bound securely to the handle with wire.   A binding of raffia covers the wire binding and completes the handle.

Hanging Basket of Rattan with Brown Band

Materials: 16 32-inch pieces of No. 2 rattan,
About 10 weavers of No. 2 rattan,
2 or 3 weavers of No. 2 brown rattan,
1 10½-inch piece of No. 4 rattan,
An awl.

This basket is specially adapted for the plants that grow in water—ivy, "wandering Jew" and others.   In it a wide-necked bottle or high glass, placed securely and hidden from view, holds a growing plant or long-stemmed flowers.   The usual sixteen-spoke centre is arranged, and on it a weaver is started in the four-row beginning. Under-and-over weaving makes a centre two inches and a quarter in diameter, the spokes are then wet and turned up with a very slight outward flare.   The sides are kept almost straight, flaring very gradually indeed for four and seven-eighths inches. They are then flared more for an inch and three-quarters, where the spokes are wet and rounded in slightly. Two weavers of the natural colour and one of brown are woven in triple twist for four rows, drawing the spokes in more and more. At the end of the fourth row the weavers are cut and the new ends started from right to left back of the spokes behind which the old ones ended. The triple twist is then woven from right to left for four rows, making the arrowhead design shown in Chapter I. These rows should be made with weavers tightly drawn, as are also three more rows of under-and-over weaving in the natural colour. The edge is then bound off and a border made as follows: The spokes are wet thoroughly. In the first row each group of spokes is brought over the next two groups on the right, under the next group and outside. If they are pulled up tightly the border will be quite open, which makes it more attractive. In the second row each group of ends is brought over the next group of spokes and inside of the basket, where it is afterward cut.

One end of the ten-and-a-half-inch piece of No. 4 rattan is run down beside a group of spokes just below the band, and the other end is pushed down beside the third group to the right to form a foundation on which the simple twisted handle described in "How to Make Baskets" is made.

Hanging Basket with Braided Handle

Materials: 16 62-inch pieces of No. 2 rattan,
              6 weavers of No. 2 rattan,
              7 or 8 weavers of No. 2 brown rattan,
              5 or 6 weavers of No. 2 black rattan,
              A piece of wire,
              A pair of pliers.

In this censer-shaped basket oxalis or other hanging plants look well. It is started with the usual sixteen-spoke centre. The four-row beginning is made and the bottom is woven into a bowl shape, with under-and-over weaving. When it is five and a half inches in diameter, two weavers of brown and one of black are woven in five rows of triple twist, drawing the sides in gradually. The sides are now brought straight up with an inch and a half of under-and-over weaving, changing the weave in every other row so as to give the appearance of double weaving. Two more rows of triple twist with two weavers of brown and one of black draw the spokes in. Four rows

HANGING BASKETS

The basket on the left has a decoration in brown. In the censer-shaped basket below the spokes form a braided handle. The oval basket on the right has bands and handle of black.

of under-and-over weaving in the natural colour
are followed by one row of triple twist in brown
and black, drawn closely. This completes the
basket. The handle is made as follows: The spokes
having been thoroughly wet,
four succeeding groups are
braided together for fourteen
and a half inches in the four-
stranded braid shown in Figure
13. The next four groups are
made into a braid and the
next and the next. These are
brought together at fourteen
and a half inches from the top
of the basket and there bound
securely with wire. Two
weavers of No. 2 brown

FIG. 13

rattan are made into small rings like the
napkin ring in "How to Make Baskets," one
with two circuits and the other with four.
These are slipped on to the handle, the
narrow one first. The ends of the handle
are wet until pliable, half of them are cut short,
and the remaining sixteen are braided into a
four-stranded plait, having four pieces in each

strand, for six and three-quarters inches.   This is
brought over into a loop and the ends, having been
very securely bound with wire to the handle, the
broadest of the brown rings is slipped up to cover
the binding.

Oval Hanging Basket of Rattan with Black Handle

Materials: 16 28-inch pieces of No. 2 rattan,
About 12 weavers of No. 2 rattan,
4 weavers of No. 2 black rattan,
1 full-length weaver of No. 4 black rattan,
An awl.

A basket that may be used for a desk scrap basket
or for flowers is made as follows: The usual
sixteen-spoke centre, with the four-row beginning
is made; pressing the weaving in at the sides and
letting it go loosely at the ends to form an oval
bottom.   When eleven rows have been woven the
bottom should measure two and a quarter by three
and a half inches.   The spokes are wet and turned
up quite straight on the sides, but flaring very
slightly at the ends.   When half an inch has been
woven two rows of black are made, followed by
three of the natural colour.   A weaver of the
natural colour and one of black make a row of

pairing, after which the under-and-over weaving in the natural colour continues for an inch and a half. The sides are still kept quite straight while the ends flare slightly. Four rows of the natural colour are woven without changing the weave, then the weave is changed and two rows are woven without changing. The weave changes again and four more rows are woven without changing. The weave is again changed and two rows woven without change. Three-eighths of an inch of under-and-over weaving is followed by six rows of triple twist with one weaver of black and two of the natural colour. Five-eighths of an inch of under-and-over weaving comes next and then a band of four rows without changing the weave, followed by a band of two without change of weave. The spokes are now wet and one row of under-and-over weaving begins to draw them in. Three rows of under-and-over weaving in black with a tightly drawn weaver are succeeded by three-quarters of an inch of under-and-over weaving, still drawing the spokes in closely. The spokes are bent back into a vertical position and half an inch more is woven. The edge is bound off and finished with this border: The spokes are wet until pliable. In the first row each group of spokes is brought back of the next group on the right and outside. In the second row each group of ends is brought over the next group of spokes, above a group of ends, and in. A handle with interlaced ends (see Chapter VI. of "How to Make Baskets") is made with a weaver of No. 4 black rattan and attached to the basket at either end, where the top band of black is woven in the basket.

Square Baskets

CHAPTER V

SQUARE BASKETS

IT is often desirable to know how to make square baskets of a durable material like rattan; so, although they are more difficult than either the round or oval baskets, and rarely as attractive, directions for making several are given in this chapter. Square baskets of palm-leaf will be found in Chapter IX.

Square Basket with Band of Green and Black

Materials: BASKET—21 22-inch spokes of No. 3 rattan,
         9 8-inch spokes of No. 3 rattan,
         4 6-inch spokes of No. 3 rattan,
         4 12-inch spokes of No. 5 rattan,
         About 8 weavers of No. 2 rattan,
         3 weavers of No. 2 green rattan,
         3 weavers of No. 2 black rattan.

COVER AND HINGE—20 18-inch spokes of No. 3 rattan,
         9 8-inch spokes of No. 3 rattan,
         4 6-inch spokes of No. 3 rattan,
         4 8-inch spokes of No. 5 rattan,
         About 5 weavers of No. 2 rattan,
         1 weaver of No. 2 green rattan,
         2 weavers of No. 2 black rattan,
         An awl.

A pliable weaver of No. 2 rattan is doubled around one of the twelve-inch spokes of No. 5, at about three inches from one end, to make the first of thirteen stitches of pairing. Eleven of the twenty-two-inch spokes of No. 3 are enclosed, one with each stitch of pairing, at about eight inches from the end of each and at intervals of three-eighths of an inch. The last stitch encloses another of the twelve-inch spokes of No. 5, at three inches from its end. The two spokes of No. 5, thus bound at either end, should be quite stiff. The other two of the same number and length should be of very pliable material. One of these is now woven under and over the long ends of the spokes, which are held by the row of pairing. A pliable weaver of No. 2 rattan is next started and woven across for three rows, passing around the outside spoke of No. 5, on either side. A pliable spoke of No. 3 rattan, twenty-two inches long, is woven across; then, bringing the weaver around the end of this spoke (instead of around the outside spoke of No. 5), three rows of No. 2 are woven and another spoke, this time a short one, of No. 3. Three more rows of No. 2 are woven and another long spoke. In this way the whole bottom is made.

When finished it should measure six by six inches. The long ends of weaver left after the spokes were bound in place with pairing are now woven around the other three sides of the bottom, in one row of pairing; this should be pressed close in to the weaving. The ends of the short spokes of No. 3 are cut close to the pairing, and the long spokes, having been wet until pliable, are turned up. Straight sides are woven with eight rows of under-and-over weaving. Three rows follow without changing the weave, then six rows more, the weave being changed with each row. Three rows of under and over weaving in black rattan are followed by three rows of green, without changing the weave. The weave is changed, and two rows of green are woven without changing the weave, and then, after changing the weave, two more. Two rows of black under-and-over weaving are followed by three of the natural colour, the edge is bound off and the following border made: The ends of the corner spokes of No. 5 are cut close to the weaving and a six-inch spoke of No. 3 rattan is inserted at each corner. The spokes are wet until pliable and each is brought back of the next two on the right. In the second row each spoke is brought over the next two spokes, above the next two ends and pressed inside, where it is cut just long enough to lie against the spoke ahead. The basket should measure six and five-eighths by six and five-eighths inches across the top. The cover is started in the same way as the basket—doubling a pliable weaver around an eight-inch spoke of No. 5 at about two and one-eighth inches from the end. A row of pairing is woven, enclosing one of the sixteen-inch spokes of No. 3 with each stitch, at a little over five inches from the end of each, for eleven stitches. These spokes should be about three-eighths of an inch apart. As in the basket, the thirteenth stitch encloses another of the eight-inch spokes of No. 5, a stiff one. A pliable eight-inch spoke of No. 5 is then woven under and over the long ends of the spokes thus bound and pressed close in to the pairing. Three rows of under-and-over weaving are followed by one of the long spokes of No. 3. Then three more rows and a short spoke. Three rows and a long spoke, three rows more, followed by three rows of under-and-over weaving in black. A short spoke of No. 3 is woven in, then six rows of under-and-over weaving in green followed by a

long spoke. Three rows of black are woven, then
a short spoke, three rows of the natural colour and
a long spoke. Three rows of weaving are followed
by a short spoke, three rows and a long spoke,
three rows and a short spoke, three rows and a
long spoke, three rows and a short spoke, three
rows and a long spoke, three rows and a short
spoke. One row of weaving in the natural colour
is followed by three in black, then a long spoke
and one more row of black. Two rows of under-
and-over weaving and a short spoke come next,
then three rows and a long spoke, three rows and
a short spoke. Two rows of under-and-over
weaving are followed by a pliable spoke of No. 5.
The ends of the weaver which bound the spokes
in pairing at the start are brought around the
other three sides in a row of pairing (here the
cover measures six and a half by six and a half
inches) and the following border is made: The
ends of the four spokes of No. 5 are cut close to
the weaving (as are the ends of the short spokes
of No. 3), and in place of them a six-inch spoke
of No. 3 is inserted at each corner. The spokes
are then thoroughly wet and each is brought under
the next one on the right and out. In the second

row each end is brought over two spokes, above
two ends and pushed inside the cover. The
hinges are made as follows: The cover is placed
on the basket so that the coloured bands will run
horizontally. At two inches from one of the back
corners of the cover the tip of a pliable piece of
No. 2 rattan is brought down between the border
and the first row of weaving, to the inside of the
basket, where it comes out between the border
and the first row of weaving, to meet the other
end. Here they are tied into a small ring and the
ends brought in and out around it till one circuit
has been made over the foundation ring. The
ends are fastened off by weaving each under and
over several spokes, between the border and the first
row of weaving in the cover. Another ring hinge
is made at two inches from the other back corner.

Square Basket of Green Rush and Rattan

Materials : BASKET—14 20-inch spokes of No. 4 rattan,
11 7-inch spokes of No. 4 rattan,
28 12-inch spokes of No. 4 rattan,
About 7 weavers of No. 2 rattan,
Fine green rush.

COVER AND HINGE—8 18-inch spokes of No. 4 rattan,
10 7-inch spokes of No. 4 rattan,
About 6 weavers of No. 2 rattan,
Fine green rush,
An awl.

In this basket a fine green rush, which is found in our swamps, is combined with No. 2 rattan in the natural colour. The spokes at one side of the bottom are held in place (as in the square basket with green and black band) with a row of pairing. First a six-inch spoke is placed on either side of a long spoke. A weaver is doubled around these spokes, at about half an inch from the end of the short ones, and seven inches from the end of the long one, and woven across in pairing, enclosing two spokes, a long one and a short one, six inches long, with each stitch. Half-inch spaces are left between them. The seventh stitch encloses three spokes, two short and a long, as did the first. Two pliable spokes, one six inches and a long one of No. 4 rattan, are woven under the end spokes over the next pair, under the next, over the next, under the next, over the next, and under the other end spokes. They are pressed close up to the row of pairing. Nine rows of under-and-over weaving in No. 2 are followed by a long spoke, woven in and out. The whole bottom is formed in this way, with six groups of nine rows of under-and-over weaving separated by six long spokes, one between each group of weaving. This should make a bottom about five by five inches. The row of pairing, which held the spokes in place at the beginning, is continued around the other three sides of the basket. The short spokes are then cut close to the weaving and the long ones are thoroughly wet. The twenty-eight twelve-inch spokes are here held, one between each of the original spokes, so that eight inches turn up and four down, and two rows of pairing bind them securely to the others. The rush is wet until pliable and an inch and an eighth is woven in triple twist up the sides of the basket. Two rows of weaving in No. 2 rattan, without changing the weave, follow, the weave is changed and two rows woven without change. The weave changes and another two rows are made without changing. Half an inch more of triple twist in rush is followed by this border: One of the two spokes at each corner is cut short; the spokes are then thoroughly wet. In the first row each spoke is brought back of the three next ones and out. In the second row each spoke is brought over the next three spokes, above the ends and inside the basket. The short ends of the extra spokes are made into a base (after wetting

them thoroughly) by bringing each end under the
next, over the next and inside the base. In
starting the cover a pliable weaver of No. 2 rattan
is doubled around two short and one long spokes,
at half an inch from the end of each short one,
and six inches from the end of the long. It is
woven across, enclosing two spokes, a long and a
short, with each stitch for six more stitches. The
eighth stitch encloses three spokes, one long and
two short. Another row of pairing is woven,
then six rows of pairing in rush and four rows of
under-and-over weaving in No. 2 rattan. The
whole cover is woven in this way. There are six
groups more of pairing in the rush, alternating with
five more groups of four rows each of under-
and-over weaving in No. 2. After the last
group of rush two rows of pairing are woven
in No. 2. This should make a cover about six
by six inches in which the spokes lie horizontally across the basket. The ends of the short
spokes are cut close to the weaving and the
long ones make a border for the ends of the cover.
Beginning with the left side of the cover, the
long spoke in the back group is cut close to the
weaving. After the spokes have been wet until

pliable, each is brought back of the next spoke and out. In the second row each is brought over the next spoke, above an end, and in. In finishing, the ends are run down between the weaving beside the back group of spokes. On the right side of the cover the border is woven from right to left so that the border on both sides will begin at the front. A hinge is made as follows: At about an inch from the centre of the basket, at the back, an end of a weaver is secured directly under the border. The long end is brought outside and across in a loop, about four inches long, to a point two inches from where it started, or an inch the other side of the centre. It goes in under the border and out through the cover just inside the back group of spokes, about an inch and three-quarters from the side of the cover. It twists around the foundation loop three times, and is brought through the cover just inside the back group of spokes, an inch and three-quarters from the other side, and returns to where it started. A third circuit makes it stronger, and the end is woven under and over several spokes below the border of the basket till it is fastened.

Large Tray-Shaped Basket

Materials: 46 34-inch spokes of No. 5 rattan,
23 18-inch spokes of No. 5 rattan,
About 16 weavers of No. 4 rattan,
About 27 weavers of No. 3 rattan,
An awl.

A perfectly square tray as large as this one would be unwieldy. The dimensions of this tray, eighteen and three-quarters by fifteen inches, make it a convenient size and shape for photographs, papers, or for gathering flowers. The method used in the other square baskets, of holding the warp spokes by a row of pairing, is followed in starting this tray. A weaver of No. 3 rattan is doubled around two thirty-four-inch spokes of No. 5 at about eight inches from an end of each. Seventeen more spokes are enclosed by as many stitches of pairing, at intervals of half an inch. A nineteenth stitch encloses two thirty-four-inch spokes of No. 5. Two rows of under-and-over weaving are made with No. 4 rattan. The weaver is cut after the first row at about two inches beyond the last spokes; it then starts again, leaving an end two inches long beyond the edge, and is woven under and over the same spokes as the first row, so that the two look like one row of double weaving. A pliable thirty-four-inch spoke of No. 5 is then woven across, leaving an end eight inches long on each side. The weaver of No. 4 rattan, coming around the end of this spoke, is woven across, around the other end of the spoke and back under and over the same spokes, as in the previous row. A pliable spoke of No. 5, eighteen inches long, follows, and so it goes the whole length of the basket; two rows of weaving are followed by a long spoke, then two rows and a short spoke, until the bottom is eighteen inches long, when twenty-five long and twenty-three short spokes will have been woven in. The bottom ends as it began, with two rows of weaving in No. 4 rattan. The ends of the weaver which bound the spokes at the beginning are carried around the other three sides in a row of pairing, and the short spokes are cut close to it. The long spokes are wet very thoroughly and turned upward at right angles with the bottom, the double spokes at the sides forming firm corners. A row of pairing is woven to draw them up into position, and then two and three-quarters inches of triple twist in No. 3, with the following border, complete it: After the spokes have been wet until pliable, each

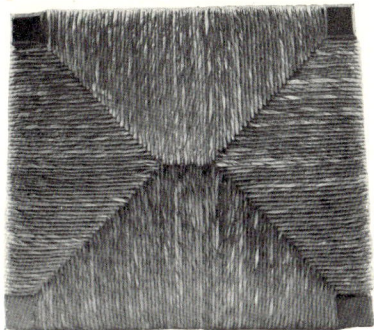

A RUSH SEAT

SQUARE BASKETS

The large tray is for photographs or letters. Below it at the left is a basket of fine green rush woven on rattan spokes. The one at the right is of rattan with a band of green and black.

is brought under the next spoke on the right, over the next, under the next and outside, where it is cut just long enough to allow it to lie against the spoke ahead.

How to Rush-Seat Chairs

CHAPTER VI

HOW TO RUSH-SEAT CHAIRS

WHEN we began to appreciate our great-grandmother's furniture, and garrets gave up their treasures of old mahogany, warming-pans and spinning-wheels, another old treasure came with them: the rush-bottomed chair. While it was lying in dust and disfavour its maker learned another craft, so that now it is almost impossible to find a workman who can rush-seat chairs. Sometimes, in out-of-the-way country places, one finds an old man who still practises the craft; but they are few, and becoming fewer. Any one with time and patience and a strong pair of hands can do it, for it is not a complicated process. The rush used is the ordinary cat-tail which grows in our marshes. It should be gathered in August, as soon as the tips begin to dry. The rush is spread on the floor of a darkened room and allowed to stay until it is thoroughly dry. The night before it is to be used it should be laid in a wet cloth, and the next morning, if it is not pliable enough to twist without cracking, it should be sprinkled with water.   One, two or three pieces may be used, according to the degree of fineness desired in the work.   One makes a very fine strand, two a medium, and three, unless it is very tightly twisted, makes quite a heavy, coarse strand.   A chair which is to be rush-seated should have simply an open frame in lieu of a seat.   A strand of rush tightly twisted is laid over the upper side of the frame, close to the right-hand corner, with its short end turning down.   The long end is brought down back of the frame, up and around the right side of the frame close to the corner, binding the short end of rush tightly. It then passes across the frame, over the left side (coming out below where it came across), up and around the upper part of the frame close to the corner.   The strand is tightly twisted as it is brought along.   It next passes down across the open frame to the lower side, where it is brought over the frame, up and back of it, around the left side close to the corner, across the open space to the lower right-hand corner (see Fig. 14).   Here it passes around the frame close to the corner,

then down over the lower side of the frame, back
and up to where it started. This simple process
is continued until the frame is filled, which, as
already said, will take time and patience. If one

FIG. 14

piece of rush is used to make the twisted strand,
new pieces are joined to it at the corners by simply
tying the two ends in a square knot. If two or
three pieces are twisted to make the strand they
should be of uneven lengths so that only one new
piece need be added at a time; the thin end of this

new length is laid with the other piece and twisted
tightly in with it.   When the frame is partially
filled (see Fig. 15), bits of rush, short waste pieces,
are stuffed into the corners, between the upper and

FIG. 15

lower layers of rush.   This is done whenever there
is room.   It will make the seat hard and firm and
improve its appearance.   An old man who is said
to make the best rush-seats on Cape Cod is author-
ity for the statement that if a piece of leather is
rubbed over the rush after it is twisted it will

give it a gloss which will add greatly to the beauty of the work. If the frame of the seat is square, the diagonal lines (formed by the crossing of the strands of rush), which come from each corner of the frame, will meet in the centre. Should it be broader from side to side than from top to bottom, the two lines on the left will meet before they reach the centre, as will those on the right. In this case the short, straight line in the centre (observable in the finished seat, see plate) will be made as follows: The strand of rush starting at the bottom will be brought up and over the upper side of the frame and the lines of rush below it; back and down to the lower side, where it is brought over and back. It then goes up again and over the upper side of the frame. This is repeated until the open space in the centre is entirely filled.

Raffia and Palm-Leaf Hats

CHAPTER VII

BEWITCHING hats are made of raffia, light and soft in texture and admitting of the greatest variety in shape. It is a material that takes colour beautifully, and one who has learned something about dyes will be able to make charming hats to match summer frocks. At the large seed stores one can buy bleached raffia, soft cream white in colour, which, though it is not strong enough for practical use in weaving baskets, makes beautiful hats. The palm-leaf hat described in this chapter is not like those made in New England, but such as one finds in the West Indies.

Raffia Hat without Frame

Materials: About ¾ of a pound of raffia,
A darning-needle, No. 1,
1⅜ yards white hat wire.

The thin ends of a bunch of raffia are cut off at about quarter of the length from each end, so that

the pieces which remain will be of uniform thick-
ness and about two feet long. The raffia is
washed in soap and water, and after it is thoroughly
rinsed is allowed to get almost dry. The strands
are cut in half and each is care-
fully smoothed out flat. They
are now ready for plaiting. In
the doll's hat described in
" How to Make Baskets " the
raffia was simply braided, no
attempt being made to keep
the plait flat, but a thick
round braid in a large hat
would make it much too heavy,

Fig. 16

so this plait will be flat and
wide.   A five-stranded plait is started (see
Fig. 16) with two vertical strands.   Across
these, at the centre, a horizontal strand is woven
from right to left, over the first and under
the second, leaving a short end turning toward
the right.   The vertical strand on the right
is doubled over horizontally across the next
one (see Fig. 17).   The plait is then turned
so that the short end points down diagonally
toward the left.   The strand which in the first

process was the vertical one on the left, is doubled
so that it first turns up diagonally to the right,
then diagonally to the left,
over the first strand and under
the second (see Fig. 18). Then
on the left the lowest strand
is turned up to the right and
brought over and under succeeding strands (see Fig. 19).
The strands are plaited up
away from the worker, taking
care always to weave on the

FIG. 17

side having the extra strand. New pieces are
added as they are needed (see Fig. 20). These ends
are cut short when the plait is finished, but should

FIG. 18

be left long enough to
be sewed firmly down
as the rows of plait
are stitched together
to form the hat. It
will take about three-
quarters of a pound
of raffia to make the

seventeen yards of plaiting which are required for
this hat. The hat is sewed with fine strands of

raffia in a No. 1 darning-needle. It is started
with two inches of the plait, making an oval
centre. The plait is coiled around so that the
edge of each new row is brought about an eighth
of an inch under the
edge of the previous
row, to which it is
sewed with a back
stitch of raffia. In
sewing, the strand is
drawn all the way
through with each in-
sertion of the needle. The top of the crown is
formed of five rows of plait, counting the centre as
one. The sides are four rows high and drawn slightly
in toward the bottom. When the brim is begun the
plait is flattened and allowed to go loosely. There
are six rows in the brim, and the last two are drawn
rather tightly as they are sewed around, so that
the edge will roll slightly. The end of the last row
is brought gradually under the previous one. The
tip is doubled in and sewed firmly under the brim
at the back of the hat. The hat is pressed as
follows: It is turned upside down on an ironing-
board and a damp cloth is laid inside the top of the

Fig. 19

crown, which is pressed with a hot iron. A damp
cloth is laid on the side of the crown, and that,
too, is pressed on the inside.   The brim is pressed
in the same way.   A row
of hat wire is sewed
against the upper side of
the last row in the brim
with small stitches in
raffia, and another row
of the plait is sewed over
it.   The upper and lower
edges of this new plait
are sewed to the corre-
sponding edges of the
last plait in the brim,
completing the hat.

Fig. 20

This hat is a broad and
rolling-brimmed sailor, but as the edge of the
brim is wired it may be bent into almost any
shape.

Raffia Hat on a Wire Frame

Materials: About 1 pound of raffia,
A darning-needle, No. 1,
A wire frame.

As a foundation for this hat a wire frame is chosen which has a low rounded crown and short curled brim in the back, growing wider on the sides until it flares up from the face in front for four inches, and rolls back for two. The plait is made with five strands as already described, and eighteen or twenty yards of it are prepared. The square end where the plait was begun forms the centre of the crown. It is bent over at five-eighths of an inch from the tip and the long end is coiled around in a second row, the edge of which comes an eighth of an inch under the edge of the centre. It is sewed with a No. 1 darning-needle, threaded with a fine strand of raffia, in back stitch, bringing the strand all the way through on the right side, then through all the way underneath. The crown is made separate from the wire frame, but is tried on it constantly, so that it will be sure to fit. When six rows have been stitched together and the crown is four and a half inches high the brim is begun. The coil of plaiting is brought around more loosely and flattened out as it is sewed. When three rows have been sewed together the brim at the back will be wide enough. Each succeeding row will have to be cut, as it gets near the back

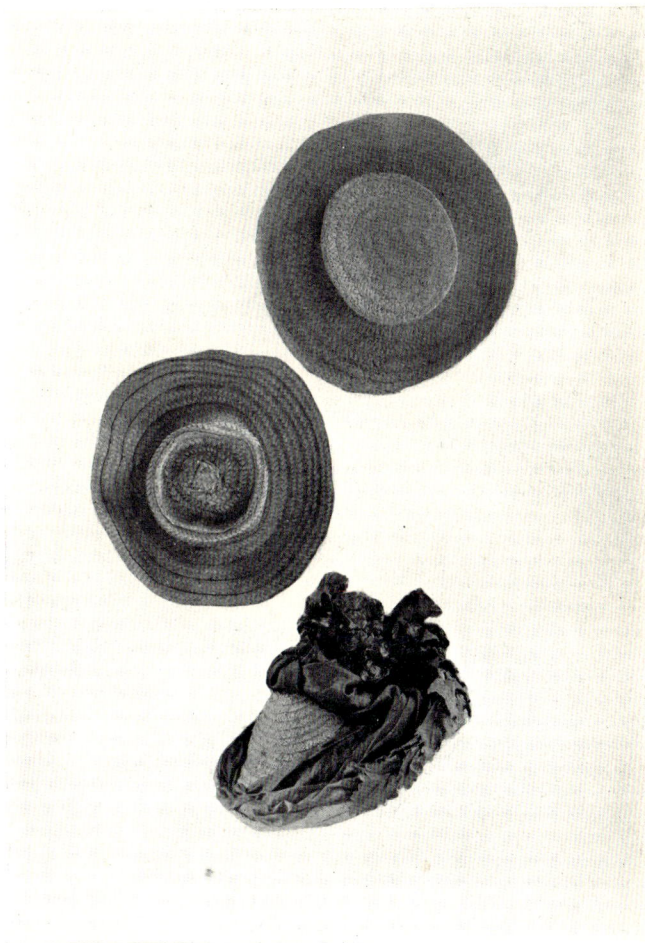

RAFFIA AND PALM-LEAF HATS

At the top of the plate is a hat made of flat plaited raffia coiled and sewed. Below it is a West Indian hat of silver top, also plaited. The trimmed hat is made on a wire frame.

and the end fitted in under the previous row, until
the side near the back is four rows wide, the side
near the front six rows, and the front seven rows.
The coil should be pulled slightly tighter as it is
drawn around to make these last rows roll. An
under-brim piece is made in the same way except
that it is one row wider at the front and sides to
allow it to roll over the edge of the brim. It is
pressed on the wrong side as already described
and attached to the under brim of the frame with
small stitches of raffia. The outer edge of this
under brim should not be fastened until the crown
and top brim are on, as it should come over the
edge of the latter. The crown and upper brim are
now pressed on the inside and put on the frame,
to which they are
caught with a stitch
of raffia here and
there. The centre of
the crown particularly
s h o u l d be firmly

FIG. 21

stitched to the centre of the wire frame. A row of
plait is brought around to cover where the upper
and under brims join, inside the rolled brim, and is
sewed on either edge with small stitches of raffia.

West Indian Palm-Leaf Hat

Materials: A bundle of silver top,
A darning-needle, No. 1.

The kind of palm leaf called silver top, which is silvery white on one side and green on the other and comes from the West Indies, is used in making

Fig. 22

the plait of which this hat is fashioned. The natives cut it into strips an eighth of an inch wide. Like the other palm leaf, it requires no wetting, but, to make it flexible, should be left in a damp place for several hours. The plait used is made with eleven strands and begins as the five-stranded one was begun, except that there are five vertical strands, which are held green side up. The long end of the weaver or horizontal strand is brought (silver side up) over the vertical strand on the right, under the next two and over the succeeding two. The first vertical strand on the right is bent over horizontally to the left and passes over the next strand, under the next two and over the next one. The next vertical strand on the right is bent hori-

zontally over one and under two. The next vertical one on the right passes over one and under one
and the next passes over one. The plait is then
turned, as shown in Figure 18. The strand which
was the remaining vertical one is bent, first up
diagonally to the right, then diagonally to the left,
passing over one, under two and over two. It
goes on in this way, always from the side having
six strands and always over one, under two and
over two. The plait is made eight yards long.
To start the centre of the crown, the end of the
plait is doubled over at an inch from where it
began, and the long end, passing from under this
square centre, is brought around, with its edge an
eighth of an inch under the
centre, in a first row. Strips of
the palm almost as fine as thread
will be found strong enough to
sew the plaits together. The
crown of the original, which was
fashioned by the brown hands of

Fig. 23

a West Indian, is made somewhat the shape of
a round hut with sloping roof. Four rows,
including the centre, make the roof-like top of
the crown and three more the straight sides.

When finished, a deep, circular crease in the crown brings it down into a shape more like the hats we wear. In starting the brim, the first row is brought more loosely and flattened out as it is stitched to the previous row. There are five rows, and the end of the last of these is brought gradually under the previous row until it reaches the middle of the back, where it is fastened securely.

Four-Stranded Plait

Materials: A bunch of silver top or palm leaf.

An attractive plait which is sometimes used to edge the brims of hats, sometimes to make whole

FIG. 24

hats or baskets, is woven as follows: Two strands of palm leaf, silver top, raffia or other flat material are used in starting. A strand of the desired width is doubled at the centre into a V shape, through which another strand is laid horizontally (see Fig. 21). The left end of this strand is bent up diagonally toward the right (see Fig. 22). The strand marked No. 2 passes over No. 1, under No. 3 and beside No. 4. No. 1 crosses over

Nos. 3 and 2 and under No. 4 (see Fig. 23). No. 1 then comes up diagonally to the left, over No. 4, under No. 2 and beside No. 3. Thus it goes on, first the outside strand on the left is brought to the right horizontally (see Fig. 24), then to the left diagonally. The outside one on the right is brought over horizontally to the left and up diagonally to the right, each as it goes passing over one strand and under the next.

Raffia Basketry

CHAPTER VIII

RAFFIA BASKETRY

ONE is constantly finding new uses for raffia. Its possibilities seem endless. Attractive even in its natural state, it is doubly so when dyed with the soft, rich vegetable colours. It is inexpensive, too, and not hard to obtain, since even in country places it may be bought of seedsmen or florists. No matter, then, what other materials we may find, there will always be a place, and a large one, for raffia in basketry.

Braided Raffia Lamp Mat

Materials: 10 yards of braided raffia,
1¾ yards of braided green raffia,
A bunch of raffia,
Several strands of green raffia,
A tapestry needle, No. 19.

A lamp mat of braided raffia in the natural colour with a design of broken circles in green is simple and good. The three-stranded braid is used. If the raffia is thick two pieces are taken for each strand, otherwise there should be three pieces in each. It is coiled and sewed like the brim of the doll's hat in "How to Make Baskets." When four rows have been made a strand of green raffia is started, the fifth coil is laid about an eighth of an inch from the previous one and attached to it with a long stitch in green. Another long stitch is made in the same place, and the raffia is brought around them twice in the opposite direction, like the open-work stitch in the raffia candy basket in "How to Make Baskets." The needle is then run along inside the braid to a point about quarter of an inch from the first stitch, where another is made. This is repeated for two rows. Eleven rows of the plain braid are sewed and then the braid is cut, at about an inch beyond the end of the last row. The end is bound tightly with raffia and sewed down on the lower side of the mat. Half an inch of the green braid is bound and sewed close down to the mat on the wrong side. The long end is coiled around and sewed to the edge of the mat, for three and five-eighths inches where it is cut, leaving an end half an inch long, which is bound and sewed against the under side of the mat. A piece of the braid in the natural colour is sewed to the edge for an inch, the ends being stitched firmly down on the wrong side. Three and five-eighths inches of the green braid are followed by an inch of the natural colour. There are four strips of each in this row. Two rows of the natural colour are followed by another row in which a strip of green braid (starting at the same place on the circumference of the mat where the previous row began) is sewed for four and five-eighths inches. A strip of braid in the natural colour an inch long follows. Another strip of the green four and five-eighths inches and another of the inch strips of the natural colour braid are sewed along. Four long strips of green and four short ones of the natural colour form this row. Three rows of braid in the natural colour follow, and the end is bound and sewed close against the lower side of the mat. A damp cloth is then laid over it on the wrong side and it is pressed with a hot iron.

Braided . Raffia Belt

Materials: A bunch of raffia.

In making this belt, as in other work with raffia, the material should be thoroughly washed with soap and water and then as thoroughly rinsed, before using. When it is almost dry six strands are selected if the raffia is thick and heavy, twelve if it is thinner and eighteen if very thin. The six strands are braided at the centre into two three-stranded braids for five and a half inches. The ends of these braids are brought together and bound securely with a strand of raffia. A long end of this strand is brought through the binding and out with the long ends of the braided strands so that there will be six strands in one group and seven in the other. These are woven into a thirteen-stranded braid in which the raffia is not kept flat but as round as in the simple three-stranded braid. The braid is woven away from the worker, taking each time the outside strand in the seven-stranded group, bringing it under one and over one to the end of the group. This makes seven strands in the opposite group. The ends of the strands are drawn rather horizontally than vertically as they are pulled up. It will be advisable, before beginning to weave the seventh strand across, to turn the strands which were the under ones in the previous row back on the braid. The seventh strand can then be brought across without weaving, and the under strands are turned up over it. Care should be taken not to draw one strand more than another, or the edge will be uneven. New lengths are added when they are needed, as in the raffia plait for hats. When the belt is the required length the ends are made into two three-stranded braids (one having the thirteenth piece in it, making two pieces in one of its strands) seven and a half inches long. Each is then tied with a knot to fasten it. The ends are fringed out for about an inch. In fastening the belt each braid is brought through the opposite braided loop and the ends are tied in a square knot.

Raffia Candle Shade

Materials: A pliable length of No. 5 rattan,
A bunch of orange raffia,
10 large white beads,
20 large black beads,
A tapestry needle, No. 19.

Candle shades made of knotted raffia are new and effective. A pliable piece of No. 5 rattan which has been whittled to a long, flat point at one end is wet and coiled into a ring eight and three-quarters inches in circumference. A tapestry needle which has been threaded with a strand of orange raffia is run through the short end of rattan,

down through the coil below, to hold the ring
together. The long end is brought around in a
lower coil which is bound to the upper one with
the Figure-of-eight stitch shown in Figure 25. A

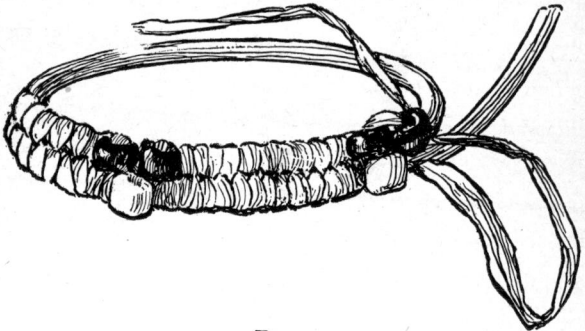

FIG. 25

group of two black beads and a white one is
bound in with the same stitch in this way. The
strand of raffia, after passing over and back of the
lower coil, is brought up over the upper one. Here
a large black bead is threaded on and bound
close against the outside of the upper coil. The
strand passes down back of the upper coil, over
the lower one, back and up, over the upper one,
down and back of it and over the lower coil, then
up back of it and over the upper coil. In returning, a large white bead is threaded on and bound

close to the lower coil. Two more stitches are made, and then, as the strand of raffia is brought up to go over the upper coil, another black bead is threaded on it and bound close to the coil. Five of these groups are made at intervals of an inch and three-quarters (measuring from the centre of each group to the centre of the next) around this upper ring. The lower ring is made in the same way but larger. It should be eighteen inches in circumference, and the groups (measuring from the centre of one to the centre of the next) are about three and five-eighths inches apart. The two rings are joined with knotting as follows: Twenty strands of raffia are knotted on to the small ring, four between each group of beads. The first row of knots is made close to the ring. At about half an inch from the first row the strands are separated and a second row is knotted, forming half of a diamond-shaped mesh. The strands are then brought straight down and knotted at an inch and a half from the previous row. They are again separated and are knotted at about half an inch from the row above, making half a diamond-shaped mesh. The ends are attached to the lower ring by sewing them through the binding several times with a tapestry needle. A brown paper pattern, cut to fit the frame which holds the shade, is now placed on it and the knotting is wet and stretched over it, to dry in shape. A lining of harmonious colour is afterward cut by the pattern, and the knotting is sewed on to it with a fine strand of raffia, above the first row of knots at the top, and below the last row at the bottom. Asbestos guards should be provided for these shades.

Raffia Lamp Shade

Materials: A piece of No. 4 rattan 3 yards long,
A piece of No. 4 rattan 5 yards 14 inches long,
A bunch of raffia,
A bunch of black raffia,
An awl,
A tapestry needle, No. 19.

A piece of No. 4 rattan three yards long is whittled to a sharp point at each end. It is then coiled into a circle eleven inches in diameter and the long end brought around and bound to it with raffia, making the joinings as neat as possible by laying the short ends along the foundation ring and covering them as the binding proceeds. A third row of rattan is laid beside the other two and

bound to them with a stitch which passes around
the second and third coils, between two stitches.
An awl will be a help in this process. When five
inches have been covered in the natural-coloured
raffia a band of black is made by bringing a piece
of black raffia over the two lower coils, back of the
upper one, over the two upper coils, back of the
lower one, and up over the two lower coils again.
Two inches are made in black, five inches in the
natural colour, two inches in black, and so on until
the ring is covered with five spaces of each. A
larger ring twenty-one inches in diameter is made
in the same way with a piece of No. 4 rattan
five yards f o u r t e e n
inches long. The bind-
ing in the natural colour
covers spaces nine inches
wide and those in black
are three and seven-
eighths inches. Forty-
two strands of raffia

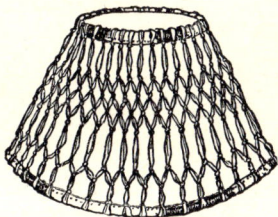

Fig. 26

are knotted on the small ring. The strands are
brought straight down and knotted together again
at two inches from the first row of knots. They
are then separated and three rows of knotting are

made in diamond-shaped meshes. The strands are again brought straight down and knotted together at two inches from the previous row, separated and knotted into two more rows of diamond meshes. The shade is then dampened and put over a paper-covered frame and the large ring attached to the loose ends of the strands.

Hat Brush and Holder

Materials: BRUSH—Short ends of raffia,
      A bunch of raffia,
      A bunch of green raffia,
      A darning-needle, No. 1.
    HOLDER—2 26-inch pieces of No. 5 rattan,
      6 large black beads,
      A bunch of raffia,
      A bunch of green raffia,
      A darning-needle, No. 1.

The thin ends of raffia left after the centre of the strands has been plaited for hats may be utilized in making a hat brush. About thirty-five of these pieces eleven inches long are bound tightly together with a strand of raffia, for an inch and a half, at about three inches from the thicker ends, which are to form the brush. The end is fastened securely by sewing it through and through the binding. Eight of these bunches are thus bound. They are then

separated into groups of four. One of these groups
is held flat and bound together, above the individual
bindings next to the long ends, with a strand of
raffia which is brought around it three times. The
strand then comes out between each bunch and
around the first binding, in the opposite direction
twice, making a vertical stitch. The second
group of four is bound in the same way. The long
and irregular ends of both groups are laid so that
they cross at the centre, making the foundation
of a handle seven and a half inches long. If they
make too thick a bunch to form a shapely handle,
some of the ends may be cut out with long
slanting cuts. The handle is bound tightly around
so that the strands are secured, the groups of four
are laid side by side and the inner bunches sewed
securely together. The handle is then covered
smoothly with a binding of green raffia. A needleful
of green raffia is secured at one side of the lower end
of the individual bindings, close to the brush ends.
It is woven under the first group, over the next
and so on, under and over back and forth across the
eight bunches four times. If this does not make the
brush firm enough, vertical stitches may be made
between the groups around this horizontal binding.

Holder.—One of the twenty-six-inch pieces of No. 5 rattan is sharpened to a long, flat point and coiled into a ring twelve and three-quarters inches in circumference, where a coarse darning-needle threaded with raffia is run through to hold the ring together. A second coil is brought around and bound to the first one with the Figure-of-eight stitch shown in Figure 25. At intervals of an inch and five-eighths six bands of green raffia are made, about half an inch wide, with the same stitch. In the centre of each of these bands a large black bead is fastened in this way: Two stitches of green are made, a black bead is then held, with the hole up, against the ring, and the strand of raffia, which is brought over the outside coil of rattan, passes down through the bead, back of the inner coil, out and over it and down through the bead again. Two more stitches of green finish the band. The end of the coil is whittled to a sharp point and bound close to the ring about an inch beyond where the first end started. A second ring is made the same size as the first with the Figure-of-eight stitch in natural-coloured raffia. At a point chosen for the top of the holder a loop to hang it by is made as follows: The Figure-of-eight stitch stops and two and a half inches of buttonhole stitch covers the outer coil. It is bent up so as to leave about an eighth of an inch between it and the inner coil. The inner coil is joined to it with the Figure-of-eight stitch for the rest of the distance around the ring. The portion of inner coil which was left bare when the outer one was covered with buttonhole stitch is now covered with the same stitch. The two rings are bound together with buttonhole stitch for an inch on either side, and the brush is slipped in between them, handle down.

Raffia Rattle

Materials: 16 26-inch spokes of No. 2 rattan,
Raffia in the natural color.

The spokes are arranged in the sixteen-spoke centre (see Fig. 1). A weaver of raffia, doubled in the centre, is woven in two rows of pairing inclosing four spokes with each stitch. The groups are divided into twos, and two rows of pairing woven. They are then separated into single spokes and the rattle formed into a bowl-shape five inches in circumference at an inch and a half from the centre. From there it is drawn in gradually until, at about two inches and a quarter from the centre, the narrowing is begun by cutting a spoke to a quarter of an inch from the weaving, whittling it to a point and binding it in with the next spoke. Three or four spokes may be cut out in the first circuit and more in subsequent ones. At three and a half inches from the centre there should be twelve spokes left. These are l a i d together and bound close- ly with raffia into a handle three inches long. Half of the spokes are then cut off. The remaining ones are cut four inches long, whittled to a point and bent over to form a loop at the end of the handle. It is bound fast to the handle and wound with raffia till it is covered. At about a quarter of an inch from the end of the binding a loop of raffia is laid on it with the loop turning down and bound in with it as the winding continues (see Fig. 27). The end of the raffia is slipped through the loop and drawn up through the binding, where it is cut short.

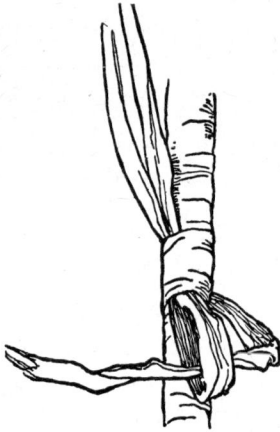

FIG. 27

Three Stitches and a Centre

Though it is sometimes possible to obtain Indian material, the preparation and use of it are difficult for unaccustomed fingers, so we turn naturally to raffia, that satisfactory substitute which is always plentiful and ready for use. A simple Indian centre may be made with rattan and raffia.

Twenty spokes of No. 2 rattan of the required length are wet until pliable. Ten vertical spokes are bound to a horizontal one, which is laid back of them, as follows: A strand of raffia is started back of the horizontal spoke, at the left of the first vertical one, with its short end turning down. The long end is brought diagonally down across the first vertical spoke, back of the lower end of it and out at the left side below the horizontal one. Here it comes up diagonally across the vertical spoke, binding the short end close to it, back of the horizontal spoke and out on the lower right side of the second vertical spoke. It then goes over diagonally to the left of the upper end of the second vertical spoke, back of the horizontal one, to the lower left side of the second vertical spoke, up across it diagonally and down back of the horizontal spoke to the right of the lower end of

the third vertical one.   In this way each of the ten
vertical spokes is bound to the horizontal one.
Another horizontal spoke is laid below the first one
and the vertical spokes are bound to it in the same
way (with a strand of
raffia in a tapestry
needle) in another row
of cross stitches. More
spokes are added, one
at a time (see Fig. 28)
until there are ten hori-
zontal spokes bound
to ten vertical ones with
a cross stitch at each
crossing of spokes. The
Thompson River Indians use a weave which
Professor Mason of the Smithsonian Institution
calls imbrication. It is beautiful as one sees
it forming a decoration in glistening white on
their baskets of cedar and spruce root, so solidly
and closely woven. The coiling stitch of the
foundation has already been described in "How
to Make Baskets." It passes around the bunch
of splints (or pieces of No. 2 rattan) and is locked
into the stitch below. In place of the bark or

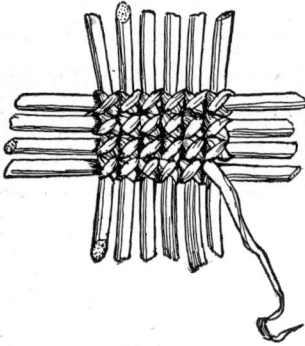

FIG. 28

grass employed by the Indians we can use a strand
of coloured raffia or a length of silver top for the
ornament. This strand is laid flat against the coil,
and its short end, turning toward the right, is caught
down with one of the foundation stitches. The
long end is then bent forward, covering the foundation stitch, and into a little pleat, which the next
foundation stitch binds close to the coil. The
coloured strand is again bent forward, covering
the stitch thus made. In this way the coil stitches
are hidden and only the ornamental band shows
(see Fig. 29). A simple stitch that looks like an
Indian one, the "Lazy Squaw" stitch, is used
from Maine to California in making raffia baskets.
It is sewed over a
coil of rattan, raffia
or cord. The smallest
possible ring is made
of an end of the founda-
tion coil and bound

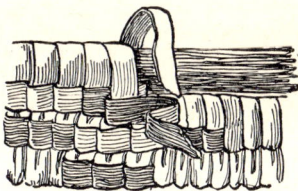

FIG. 29
(Courtesy of Prof. Otis T. Mason.)

tightly over and over
with raffia for two rows. In the third row the
needle passes out under the previous coil, over that
coil and the new one, around the new coil once
(making a long and a short stitch), down and out

under the previous coil (see Fig. 30). Designs in colour are easily worked on baskets made with this stitch, and it may be further varied by an occasional row of the openwork coiled stitch

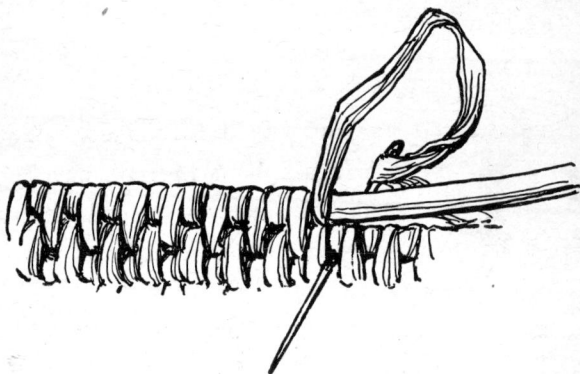

FIG. 30

described in Chapter VIII. of "How to Make Baskets." Another coiled stitch is used—sometimes to form the bottom, sometimes in bands on baskets made with the "Lazy Squaw" stitch. A piece of fine cord about the size of No. oo rattan is laid above the coil of rattan and bound in with it, in the first row. In the next and subsequent rows the needleful of raffia is brought around the new coil, out and then back (away from the worker), under or through the cord in the coil below (see Fig. 31). It is then brought out toward the worker under the new coil and, passing around it, comes out again toward the worker, when it is run back in the opposite direction under the cord in the lower coil.

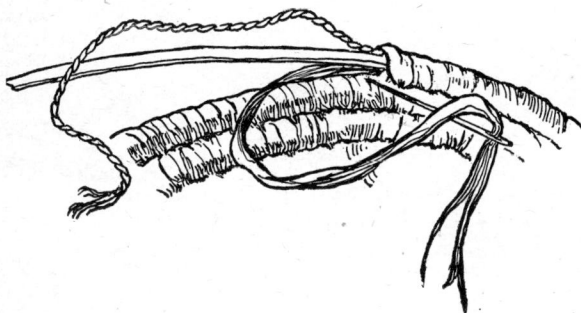

FIG. 31

Raffia Basket for Collar Buttons

Material: 2 weavers of No. 2 rattan,
        A bunch of olive green raffia,
        A bunch of pale yellow raffia,
        A bunch of black raffia,
        A tapestry needle, No. 19.

A pliable end of a weaver of No. 2 rattan is wound with olive green raffia, threaded in a No. 19 tapestry needle, and coiled into the smallest possible ring. A second coil is bound to the first and then the basket is made in the "Lazy Squaw" stitch (see Fig. 30). On the fifth row a strand of yellow is started, one long stitch of yellow is made and the yellow strand is laid along the coil of rattan and covered by the stitches in olive green. At a distance of half an inch from the first one another long yellow stitch is made and the yellow strand is carried along on the coil of rattan, covered by olive-green stitches for another half inch, where a long yellow stitch is made.

FIG. 32

There will be five of these stitches, at intervals of half an inch, in this row.   In the next row one long yellow stitch is made to the right and left of each one in the previous row with one olive green stitch between them.   In making these yellow stitches the olive-green strand is carried along under them, as already described.   This starts the design, a five-petaled flower in yellow outlined on an olive-green background (see Fig. 32).   In the next row a long yellow stitch is made to right or left (as the case may be) of each yellow stitch in the previous row, continuing the design. In the next row, on the left of the pattern, one long yellow stitch followed by two short ones is made, to the right of the long yellow stitch in the previous row; and on the right of the pattern two short stitches and a long one are made, at the left of the long yellow stitch in the row beneath. This brings the lines of the petal shape closer together. In the next row, beginning at the left of the pattern, two short yellow stitches are made above the two in the previous row, then one long, three short, one long and two short, which will close the end of each petal. In the next row a short yellow stitch is made above the first long yellow stitch in the previous row, then a long stitch, a short one, another long and a short one. Each petal is continued in this way. In the last row of the pattern a long yellow stitch is made to the right of each short one on the left of the pattern, in the previous row. A short stitch and another long one complete the design. If it becomes necessary to add a second piece of rattan before the basket is finished, the old and new ends are sharpened to a long, flat point and bound as one. Two rows of green are made which finish the bottom. The next row of coiling is brought above and a little outside the previous one. Four rows of green, followed by two of black, flare quite decidedly. Then four rows of yellow are made still flaring. Two rows of black brought one above the other make a straight-sided edge. The end of the coil is whittled into a long flat point for about two and a half inches, which when bound down to the previous row hardly shows where it is finished.

Covered Raffia Basket

Materials: Two or three lengths of No. 3 rattan,
A bunch of raffia,
A bunch of brown raffia,
A tapestry needle, No. 19.

A collar button basket of coiled rattan wound with raffia is made like the raffia candy basket in "How to Make Baskets." The No. 3 rattan, however, makes a somewhat finer coil, and the bands of golden brown in the cover form a decoration which, though simpler, is quite as effective as the design on the candy basket. The bottom is made in the openwork coiled stitch for twelve rows. Straight sides ten rows high are made, and the eleventh row, coming inside the tenth, forms a little edge upon which the cover rests. The cover has three rows of plain openwork coiling, counting the centre as one, and then the uncovered coil is brought close to the last row and a band of brown in Figure-of-eight stitch (see Fig. 25) is made. Eight rows of open-work coiling are followed by a border of the Figure-of-eight stitch in brown. The hinge is made in the same way as the one on the candy basket.

Raffia Basket with Dragon-Fly Design

Materials: About 20 weavers of No. 2 rattan,
2 pieces of No. 6 flat rattan 14½ inches long,
A bunch of raffia,
A bunch of sage-green raffia,
A bunch of black raffia,
Several strands of pale-yellow raffia,
A tapestry needle, No. 19.

Twenty spokes sixteen inches long are cut from No. 2 rattan and when they have been thoroughly wet are bound in this way. They are separated into two groups of ten each. One of these groups is laid on a table vertically and the others are placed across them horizontally. A strand of

raffia is doubled around the upper left-hand vertical
spoke and the ends are brought together and down
over the horizontal spokes, to the right of the
lower end of the same spoke. The strand goes

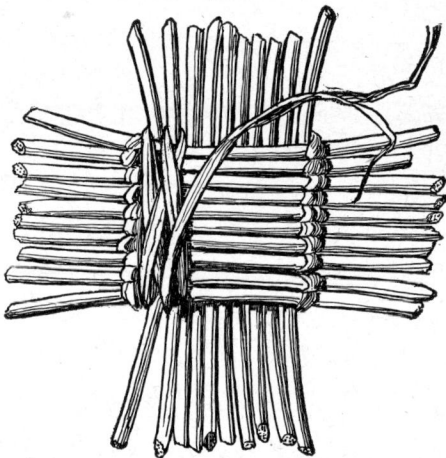

Fig. 33

back of this spoke out on the left and up to the
right of the upper end of the second vertical one.
It passes back and out on the left, down over the
horizontal group and around the lower end of the
same spoke from right to left. So it goes on until
all the vertical spokes have been bound. Care
must be taken to keep the horizontal ones flat and

in place. The centre is then turned over and the
horizontal spokes are bound in the same way (see
Fig. 33). The basket is woven in pairing, adding
new spokes from time to time as they are needed.
A three-inch bottom is made and then the spokes
are wet thoroughly and brought up in a decided
flare, for seven-eighths of an inch. The basket
should now measure about fifteen and a quarter
inches in circumference. A strand of black raffia
is doubled around a spoke to make one stitch of
pairing. At intervals of two and a half inches one
of these stitches is made, until there are five. The
ends of each black strand are left loose. In the
next row these ends are brought around the same
spoke, to make a stitch just above each black
one in the last row, and so on for fifteen rows to
make the body of the dragon-fly. At the end of
the eighth row the spokes are wet and the sides are
brought in gradually more and more, cutting out
spokes now and then (see directions for raffia
rattle). On the thirteenth row from the beginning
of the body, at three-quarters of an inch either
side of it, one stitch in sage green is made—the
beginning of the dragon-fly's wings (see Fig. 34).
In the next row four stitches in green are made in

each group, one on the outer side and two toward
the body of the dragon-fly, with one between them.
In the next row each group has eight stitches, one
stitch on the outer side and three toward the body,
with four between. In the next row there are

FIG. 34

twelve stitches, one stitch beyond those in the last
row on the outer side and three toward the body,
with eight between.

The green stitches on the outside of each group
come next to those in the adjoining one, and those
on the inside adjoin the black stitch which forms
the body. In the next row there are eleven green
stitches in each group. The group starts, on the
outside, one stitch nearer the body than in the

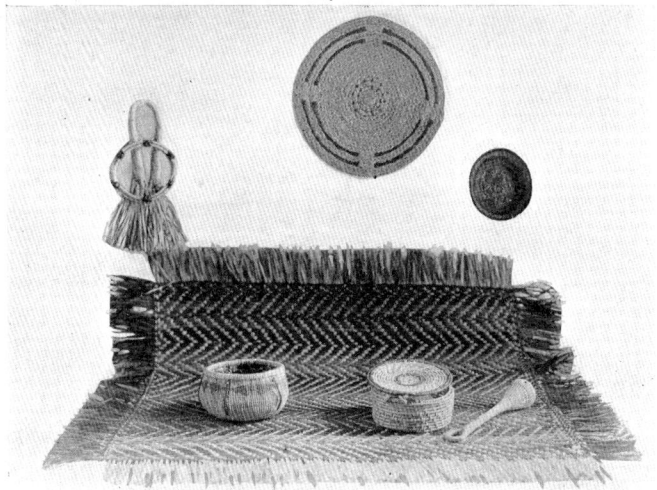

RAFFIA BASKETRY

On the left is a hat-brush and holder of green and the natural colour ; black beads form the decoration. The braided mat above has a design in green. The basket on the right is in "Lazy Squaw" stitch. Below it, on the woven mat, is a rattle. The covered basket is for collar buttons. A design of dragon-flies is woven into the one beside it.

PALM-LEAF BASKETRY

An envelope-shaped basket is shown on the left. Above and in the centre is a hanging basket. Below and to the right is a basket for collars and cuffs and beside it is a traveling case for a glass.

previous row, leaving room for two stitches of the natural colour, which are made between each dragon-fly and the next one. Nine stitches are made in each group, on the next row, and the tips of the dragon-fly's wings again touch. On the inner side there are three stitches of the natural colour between the group of green and the body. The next row is the last in which there is any green. There are six stitches in each group, beginning one stitch nearer the body than those in the previous row. There should be five stitches of the natural colour adjoining the body. The head of each dragon-fly is started in the next row. One stitch of black to the left of the black one in the previous row is followed by one of pale yellow and another of black. In the next row five black stitches are made, one above each of the yellow ones in the dragon-flies' heads. This finishes the design. Two rows of pairing in the natural colour are woven. Every other spoke is cut close to the weaving, and the alternate ones are whittled to a flat point about two inches long. They are wet until pliable and each is brought over the next one and in. The end of each spoke is cut just long enough to lie against the one ahead. Two pliable pieces of No. 6 flat rattan fourteen and a half inches long are shaved thin at either end and laid one on the outside and one inside of the border. An over-and-over stitch in raffia binds them together, passing under the last row of pairing. This makes a smooth, firm finish for the edge.

Palm-Leaf Basketry

CHAPTER IX

Palm-Leaf Basketry

West Indian palm leaf, glossy and smooth in texture, in colour pale yellow or green, makes charming baskets. It is flexible and soft, and does not need to be wet; indeed, water destroys the gloss, which is one of its chief attractions. If in our climate it becomes too dry to work without cracking, it may be left in a damp place—by an open window, for instance, on a rainy day—until the fibres become pliable. Each bundle of palm leaf contains the leaves of a single plant which vary in width from a quarter to five-eighths of an inch. In all the baskets described in this chapter the starting point is a simple mat of under-and-over weave, made like the paper mats in kindergartens. In laying the warp strands on a table, or other flat surface, the pointed end of one is turned up, then the butt end of the next, and so on, the butt and pointed ends alternating. The same method is followed in weaving the woof strands.

Traveling Case for Glass

Materials: 24 lengths of palm leaf ⅜ of an inch wide,
1 7½-inch piece of palm leaf ⅜ of an inch wide.

A light basket case to hold a small glass in
traveling makes an acceptable gift. Care should
be taken in selecting the twenty-four pieces of
palm leaf to have them as nearly uniform in width
as possible. To insure the cover and case being
of the same size, the twenty-four pieces are thoroughly mixed and then separated into two bunches
of twelve each.

Four pieces of palm leaf are laid on a table, the
first piece with sharp end up, the second with the
butt end, and so on alternately. Four pieces are
woven across, as a paper mat is made, then two
more in either direction, pressing them closely
together. Beginning at any side of the mat, the
under pieces are bent sharply forward over the
edge. The same process is followed on a side at
right angles with the first one. The mat is turned
over so that what were the upper ends of those
two sides may become the lower, and these are in
turn bent forward over the edge. With the other
two sides the method is the same, and as there is

now something to pull against the mat is made close and even. When finished it should look like Figure 35. A corner of the mat is held in each hand and bent up so that a crease is made in the middle of the side. The first strand on the right of this crease (which is to form a corner of the basket) is bent over to the left, crossing three strands. The strand that turns down is brought up over it. When the weaving strand has crossed the last of the three, whichever is the under strand is bent over the upper one. The end of the upper one follows it around and the two

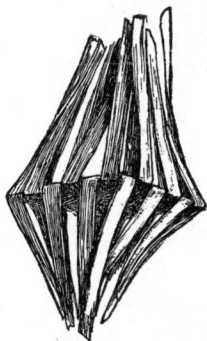

FIG. 35

are pressed into a sort of horn-shaped fastening (see Fig. 36) which holds the weaving. The first strand on the left of the crease is bent over to the right; the one that turns down is brought across it. The under strand is bent over the upper one, and the end of the upper strand following it around is pressed into the horn-shaped fastening. The same process is followed in making the other corners, starting at the centre of each side. This brings each corner of the original mat up in the middle of the side of the basket, while new corners are formed at the middle of each of the original sides. In all these palm-leaf baskets the crossing strands are of equal stiffness so that there is neither spoke or weaver. The weaving is done with both hands, o n e strand being bent over or under the next one as the case may be. When all four corners have been made there will be two l o o s e strands above e a c h

FIG. 36

corner. These cross, the right under or over the left. The end of the under one is now bent over, and the upper one, coming around back of the under, is pressed into the horn-shaped fastening (see Fig. 36). When all four pairs of strands are fastened in this way there will be an unbroken line of horn-shaped fastenings around the edge of the basket (see Fig. 37). Two fastenings are undone and the left

strand of the pair on the right is woven under or
over the next strand to the left, fastening the two
as already described. The next fastening on the
right is released, and the left strand of the new
pair crosses under or over the right one of the
previous pair. Thus it goes on around the basket,
making one row. Three fastenings are released,
and each strand, in
turn starting with the
left one of the pair on
the right, is brought
across the two next
strands over or under,
as the case may be.
This will make the

FIG. 37

sides two rows higher. One row more is
woven and the edge is finished as follows:
The upper strand of each pair, which points
up to right or left, is turned and brought diagonally down in the same direction as it pointed
up, under or over the next strand and the following
one, drawing it tightly. The strands which point
up in the opposite direction are turned and brought
diagonally down in the same way and pulled
tightly, crossing three strands (see Fig. 38). The

ends are cut close to the last strand under which they pass. The cover is started as the basket was and woven three rows high. The edge is finished in the same way except that after the upper strands are woven down, those that point up in the opposite direction are turned and brought down under one strand.

FIG. 38

Each end is then turned and brought diagonally down in the opposite direction under the next strand, making an ornament shaped like an inverted pyramid (see Fig. 39). With the ends of the same strands a second row of these ornaments is made below the first one. In a third row one of the ornaments is made at the middle of each side. Each end is cut close to the edge of the last strand it went under. In making the handle a piece of palm leaf three-eighths of an inch wide and seven and a half inches long is twisted for four inches, and the ends are attached to diagonally opposite corners of the cover by running

them under and over several strands in a direction
at right angles with the handle. The edge of the
basket and cover should
be rubbed inside and
out with a glass bottle
until they are smooth.
If the cover does not
fit as well as it should

FIG. 39

it may be stretched slightly, while the edge of
the basket may be made smaller by encircling
it with the fingers and pressing it in evenly.

Basket for Collars and Cuffs

Materials: 64 lengths of palm leaf 9-16 of an inch wide.
8 10-inch pieces of palm leaf ½ inch wide.

A square basket for collars and cuffs is made in
the same way as the traveling case for a glass.
It is, however, much larger, the material being
nine-sixteenths of an inch wide, and there are sixteen
strands each way. Half of the sixty-four strands
are put away to make the cover. Sides seven rows
high are woven, the edge is then finished as already
described and rubbed smooth with a glass bottle
inside and out. The cover is woven as the basket

was except that it is five rows high. The edge is finished by weaving the upper ends diagonally down, in the same direction they turned up, across three strands, while the under ends are brought down in the same way, under one strand. They are then turned and brought diagonally down in the opposite direction, making a row of orna-ments like those on the small b a s k e t . Another row is made below the first one, and then a third in which there is an ornament on every other square. Eight r o s e t t e s are woven, one at each corner of the top of the cover and one on each side of the cover, at the middle of it and near the top. These are made as follows: Four squares or stitches of the cover are chosen on which to place the rosette. An end of a ten-inch piece of palm leaf half an inch wide is started (see Fig. 40) by running it down diagonally under the stitch on the right.   The long end is turned and brought

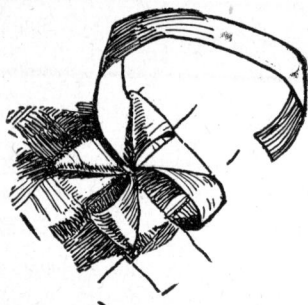

FIG. 40

down through the upper stitch. Turning, it comes down under the stitch on the left. It is then turned and brought diagonally up through the lower stitch, turned again and brought up under the stitch on the right, completing the rosette. The end is cut close to the last stitch it went under.

Hanging Basket of Palm Leaf

Materials: 24 lengths of palm leaf ½ an inch wide,
2 lengths of palm leaf ⅜ of an inch wide,
A darning-needle, No. 1,
Several strands of raffia.

A canoe-shaped hanging basket of palm leaf may be used for knitting or for flowers. It would make an ideal May basket. A large mat is woven of twenty-four lengths of palm leaf half an inch wide; twelve each way. The under strands on adjoining sides are bent up. The mat is turned, and the strands which were the over ones are bent up in the process already described (see Fig. 35). The outer strands on the four sides of the mat are sewed securely to the strands they cross with small stitches in raffia. Two of the corners are turned up to form the sides of the basket, while the other two come at either end of the bottom. The ends of those strands which turn to the right are all brought up together for about five inches and sewed through and through with a strong darning-needle threaded with raffia (see plate). Those on the left are secured in the same manner and the ends are cut neatly. A handle is made as follows: A length of palm leaf three-eighths of an inch wide is bent at one end into two loops which are sewed to an end of the basket. Another length is bent into one loop and secured at the same place, while the long ends of both are brought over to the opposite end of the basket. The end of the strand which was made into two loops here forms one and is sewed to the basket, while the end of the other strand forms two loops which are stitched through and through the basket with raffia.

Flat Palm-Leaf Basket

Materials: 32 lengths of palm leaf ½ an inch wide,
2 lengths of palm leaf 7-16 of an inch wide.

A flexible envelope-shaped basket of palm leaf makes a convenient case for handkerchiefs or photographs in traveling. The thirty-two lengths of half-inch-wide palm leaf are mixed and separated into two groups of sixteen each. One group is put away to make the cover. The basket is started with a mat centre which is woven with sixteen strands, eight each way. The process described in the directions for the traveling case for a glass are followed (see Fig. 35). The mat is then turned, so that the strands run diagonally, and bent across the centre. This will make a corner come at either end of the bottom. The other corners are turned up at the centre of the back and front of the basket. The lower end of the outside strand on the left of the front is turned a n d brought up beside its own pre-vi o u s row to the centre and there fastened, as in Figure 41. The under strands are turned up over it. The long end of the outside strand on the right is brought up to the centre and fastened in the same way. The basket is then turned over and the lower end of the outside strand on the left is brought up to the centre and fastened, as is the one on the right. This will

Fig. 41

leave several pairs of loose strands at either end of the basket. The next strand on the left of the front is woven up until it is on a line with those already secured, where it is fastened. The next strand on the right is woven up and fastened on a line with the others. The basket is turned over and the next strand on the left is woven up as far as the others, as is the next one on the right. In this way the corners are filled up, and when there is an even row of fastenings all the way around the basket the weaving proceeds as in the square baskets. The sides are ten rows high, and the edge is finished as already described. The cover is started with the sixteen remaining lengths of palm leaf and woven in the same way as the basket. The sides are eight rows high. The edge is finished, and a rosette is made (see Fig. 40) in the middle of the cover. Another rosette is made in the middle of the basket between the third and fourth rows from the bottom, and there may be two to correspond on the reverse side of the basket.

Some Natural Dyes and
Unusual Materials

CHAPTER X

SOME NATURAL DYES AND UNUSUAL MATERIALS

THERE is a fascination about colouring one's own material that only one who has proved it can understand. As an artist mixes his colours, one dye after another is tried until at last a fortunate blending gives the desired shade. Solid extracts of vegetable dyes are sold which simplify the process; or, if one lives in the country, hedgerow dyes are plentiful for those who have eyes to see and patience to use them. If one does much dyeing, rubber gloves are almost a necessity, and a brass preserving kettle will be found useful. If small quantities of material are dyed at a time half-worn basins or saucepans of medium size will do. Wash the rattan and raffia, especially the latter, in soap or soda and water and rinse thoroughly before dyeing. One of the secrets of even colouring is to boil the dye slowly, leaving the material in it for hours. In this way full deep colours will be obtained even on rattan.

Indian Red.—A beautiful shade of Indian red is made by boiling the material slowly for six hours in the following solution. Two tablespoonfuls of cutch extract and a small crystal of bluestone (about as much as would go on a ten-cent piece) dissolved in one quart of boiling water.

Green from Indigo and Fustic.—Mordant the material to be dyed with alum (three ounces of alum dissolved in a quart of water), and dye in a solution of one tablespoonful of indigo and a small crystal of copperas in one quart of boiling water. When the desired depth of colour is obtained remove the material, wash the loose dye from it and dye in a fustic bath (one quart of water in which one tablespoonful of fustic has been dissolved) to the shade required. Instead of fustic, bark extract may be used. If a brighter shade is needed, add one or two tablespoonfuls of alum mordant to the bath.

Olive Green.—Soak the rattan or raffia in water, then in one quart of water in which one tablespoonful of copperas has been dissolved, for half an hour. Boil in a fresh bath of one tablespoonful of bark extract, half a teaspoonful of indigo and one-quarter of a teaspoonful of logwood to one quart of water.

Dark Bluish Green.—Soak the material in a bath composed of one tablespoonful of copperas in one quart of water for half an hour. Then boil in a fresh bath of one quart of water in which one tablespoonful of bark extract, three quarters of a teaspoonful of indigo and a piece of logwood extract the size of a pea have been dissolved. Let it simmer for several hours or until the desired shade is obtained. The same proportion of dye in two quarts of water will give light shades.

Dark Red.—A good dark red is made with three-quarters of a teaspoonful of logwood extract, one-quarter of a teaspoonful of fustic extract, two tablespoonfuls of cochineal, two tablespoonfuls of stannous chloride and one-quarter of a teaspoonful of cream of tartar, in one quart of water. Boil slowly for several hours.

Orange.—A beautiful orange may be made with one tablespoonful of orange fustic, one-quarter of a teaspoonful of cochineal, two tablespoonfuls of stannous chloride, one-quarter of a teaspoonful of alum in one quart of water. Boil slowly until the colour is a little deeper than you wish, as it will dry lighter.

Yellow Brown.—Boil the material slowly in the following solution for several hours. One tablespoonful of cutch extract to one of fustic in one quart of water.

Olive Brown from Cutch.—To one tablespoonful of cutch extract allow one tablespoonful of fustic and one-quarter of a teaspoonful of logwood. Dissolve in one quart of water. The material should boil slowly in this bath for several hours.

Brown from Madder.—In one quart of water dissolve one to two tablespoonfuls of madder. Do not allow it to boil, but leave the material in it for five or six hours, just below the boiling point.

Hedgerow Dyes.—In a quaint old English book on dyeing one reads that "The leaves of almond, peach or pear trees give yellows which serve to make green shades if boiled with alum and tartar." This, too, is interesting: "A stuff dyed in the King's blue, well scoured, then boiled with four parts of alum and one of tartar, takes a fine deep green of the shade of a duck's wing, but it must be boiled for two hours in a liquor with a sufficient quantity of the root of sharp-pointed dock, grossly bruised. This root, which grows in every hedge and field, is a good acquisition, for . . . it produces an infinity of shades from straw colour to a pretty, fine olive. These shades stand all manner of proof."

Yellow from Dock Root.—Gather the roots of yellow dock and allow them to get thoroughly dry. Break them into small pieces; wash and soak for several days in one quart of water in which half a tablespoonful of washing soda has been dissolved. Boil the material in the same water very slowly for five or six hours. This will give reddish shades of yellow. For brighter shades add half a teaspoonful of alum.

Olive Brown from Walnut Bark.—To two pounds of fresh black walnut bark add two table-spoonfuls of washing soda and about a cup of rock alum. Cover with boiling water. Boil the material in it slowly for about twenty-four hours. Stir and turn the material from time to time and add more water if it boils away. When the material is the desired shade remove from the dye and rinse in cold water.

Yellow Brown from Oak Bark.—Soak one pound of oak bark in one quart of water in which a lump of washing soda about the size of a large egg has been dissolved, for three days, or if dark shades are required, for a week. The material to be dyed is also washed in water with soda in it. It is then boiled with the oak bark until it is the desired shade. If a small quantity of alum is added the brown becomes brighter.

Olive Brown from Sumac.—Soak one pound of the cone-shaped fruit of the sumac in one quart of water, in which one tablespoonful of washing soda has been dissolved, for several days. The material should simmer in this for twenty-four hours. If the water boils away add a little more.

Unusual Materials.—There is a silvery white Japanese fibre that makes wonderfully beautiful baskets. It is strong and may be employed successfully in pairing where the strands can be twisted, but as it frays slightly it cannot be used in sewed baskets. Another fibre of the same colour is silver top, a relative of the more prosaic palm leaf. It comes from the West Indies, where it is plaited and sewed into hats (see Chapter VII.) and soft baskets. The silver side is slightly fuzzy and soft, while the reverse looks almost like cane, it is so shiny and smooth. This smooth side is sometimes pale-green, sometimes a light-brown. It is successfully used in the triple braid and in any weave where a flat material is required. The smooth side may be separated from the silver one with a sharp knife. This makes it an ideal material for coiled baskets, tough and strong and agreeable in colour. A wood fibre that is used to tie up tobacco comes in pale yellow and orange. It is lacey in texture and quite brittle until dampened, when it becomes pliable and is plaited into a flat braid for hats. The Indians use slender, tough roots of cedar and spruce in many of their baskets. These may be found just below the ground after the tree has been cut down. They sometimes grow five feet long and are easily split through the centre. Then there are the rushes: Cat-tails which are gathered in August, and the fine grass-like rush with a porous centre which is found in marshy places on the Atlantic coast; these are used for baskets. In rush-seating chairs cat-tail is an excellent substitute for imported rush.

Covered Basket of Plaited Silver Top

Materials: A bundle of silver top,
A darning-needle, No. 1.

This flexible covered basket of plaited silver
top is quite unlike any others we have made.
The five-stranded plait described in Chapter VII.
is sewed with fine fibres of silver top. The bottom
of the basket is coiled and sewed like the palm-
leaf hat for five rows, counting the centre. Straight
sides seven rows high are made. The cover is
coiled and sewed in the same way for five rows.
Three rows form the sides. A soft handle of
braided silver top having two or three pieces in
each of its three strands is made. It is twenty-
four inches long, and starts at the centre of the
basket, where an end is sewed securely. The long
end passes up around the side of the basket, to
which it is stitched, through the fifth row from
the centre of the cover, down again through
the fifth row from the centre on the opposite
side of the cover. It is sewed to the side
of the basket until it meets the other end at
the bottom of the basket, where it is stitched
firmly.

Unfinished Basket of Rattan and Silver Top

Materials: 24 30-inch spokes of No. 2 rattan,
48 15-inch spokes of No. 2 rattan,
About 5 weavers of No. 2 rattan,
A bundle of silver top,
An awl.

The unfinished basket in the plate shows a centre which is an elaboration of the sixteen-spoke centre shown in Figure 2.
It is s t a r t e d in the same way, except that t h e r e are two more groups of four each, one of which is woven vertically, the other horizontally under and over alternate groups (see Fig. 42). A weaver is

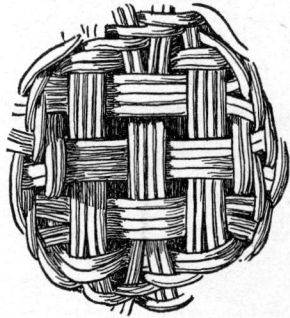

FIG. 42

started under the left end of the upper horizontal group, is brought over the next group, under the next, and so on for two rows. The spokes are then separated into twos, and the weaver is brought under a pair in one group and the adjoining pair in the next. It passes over the remaining pair in that group and

the next pair in the following one. In this way
the bottom, three and a half inches in diameter,
is woven. Extra spokes are inserted, two between
each original pair. These are wet and turned up,

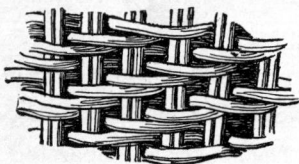

flaring outward. The
same stitch is con-
tinued up the sides for
an inch, the weaver
p a s s i n g over two
groups and under two
(see Fig. 43). Here the

FIG. 43

triple braid is started with silver top and one
row is woven. The spokes are separated into
ones, and four more rows of triple braid are made.
The basket may be finished at any desired height.

Basket of Rattan and Silver Top

Materials :   16 22-inch spokes of No. 2 rattan,
32 10-inch spokes of No. 2 rattan,
2 weavers of No. 2 rattan,
About 4 weavers of No. 2 black rattan,
About 2 weavers of No. 2 Indian red rattan,
A bunch of silver top,
An awl.

A basket with a round bottom and square
sides is unusual. This one may serve as a jardinière

for a small plant. A sixteen-spoke centre is started
(see Fig. 2) and woven to a diameter of two and
seven-eighths inches, when two additional spokes
are inserted between each pair. The spokes are
wet until pliable and turned up to form flaring
sides. The groups are separated into twos and a
row of triple braid is woven in silver top. Two
rows of pairing, with a weaver of black and one
of Indian red, are made. The spokes are separated
into ones and an inch of triple braid is woven in
silver top. The sides should then be pressed
into a square shape and kept in this way by con-
stant pressure. A row of triple twist in No. 2
black rattan is followed by five rows of silver top
in the stitch shown in Figure 43. A row of triple
twist in black rattan is made, and the spokes are
wet until pliable and rounded in. Three-quarters of
an inch of silver top in triple braid is followed by
this border: the spokes are brought together
into groups of two. Each of these groups is
brought over the next three groups on the right,
under the next two, over the following group,
and in, where the ends are cut after the border is
finished.

Basket of Green Rattan and Japanese Fibre

Materials: 16 12-inch pieces of No. oo pale green rattan,
50 6-inch pieces of No. oo pale green rattan,
About 4 weavers of No. oo pale green rattan,
A bunch of Japanese fibre,
4 lengths of silver top,
An awl.

An exquisitely fine basket is woven in pairing with glistening white Japanese fibre on spokes of No. oo rattan in pale green.   It is started with the sixteen-spoke centre shown in Figure 1, with the four-row beginning.   A bottom an inch and three-sixteenths in diameter is woven with a weaver of No. oo green rattan.   Extra spokes are inserted, two between each of the original pairs, and four rows more are woven.   The spokes are wet thoroughly and turned up with a decided flare.   The groups are separated into ones with pairing in Japanese fibre for three-eighths of an inch.   They are then brought together into twos and a row of pairing in No. oo green rattan is woven.   A row of under-and-over weaving in silver top (silver side out) is made.   Another row of pairing in No. oo green follows.   Extra spokes are inserted one between each of the under pairs.   The spokes are again separated into ones, and three rows of pairing in the Japanese fibre are woven. The spokes are brought together into twos, and a row of pairing in No. oo green rattan is followed by a row of under-and-over weaving in silver top, the sides flaring. A row of pairing in No. oo green rattan is made, and between each of the under groups of spokes one spoke is inserted. The spokes are separated into ones. Five-eighths of an inch of pairing in Japanese fibre is woven, the sides still flaring. A row of pairing in No. oo green rattan draws the spokes into pairs. A row of under-and-over weaving in silver top is followed by another row of pairing in the No. oo. The spokes are separated into ones, and three-quarters of an inch of pairing in Japanese fibre draws them in more and more. Occasional spokes are cut out as in the raffia rattle. The spokes are brought together into twos, wet until pliable and bent up straight. A row of pairing in No. oo green is made. A row of under-and-over weaving in silver top is followed by one of pairing in No. oo green. The ends of the weavers are run under a pair of spokes inside the basket to fasten them. The spokes are then cut close to the last row of pairing, which completes it.